"Two Thoughts"

INFINITE
BOOKS

www.infinitebooks.com

© 2024 by O'Shaughnessy Ventures LLC
ALL RIGHTS RESERVED

Paperback Edition

CREATIVE DIRECTOR:
Saeah Wood

PRODUCTION & EDITORIAL MANAGER:
Amy Reed

EDITORIAL:
Amy Reed, Christa Evans, Matthew Hoover

DESIGN:
Ivica Jandrijević

ILLUSTRATION:
Elizabeth Evey

LCCN:
2024915998

ISBN:
978-1-964378-00-8 *(Hardcover)*
978-1-964378-01-5 *(Paperback)*
978-1-964378-02-2 *(E-book)*
978-1-964378-09-1 *(Audiobook)*

INFINITE
BOOKS

O'Shaughnessy Ventures LLC
Greenwich, CT
www.infinitebooks.com
contact@infinitebooks.com

OTTERPINE
otterpine.com

"Two Thoughts"

A Timeless Collection of Infinite Wisdom

Jim O'Shaughnessy with Vatsal Kaushik

To the enduring spirit of inquiry and dissent

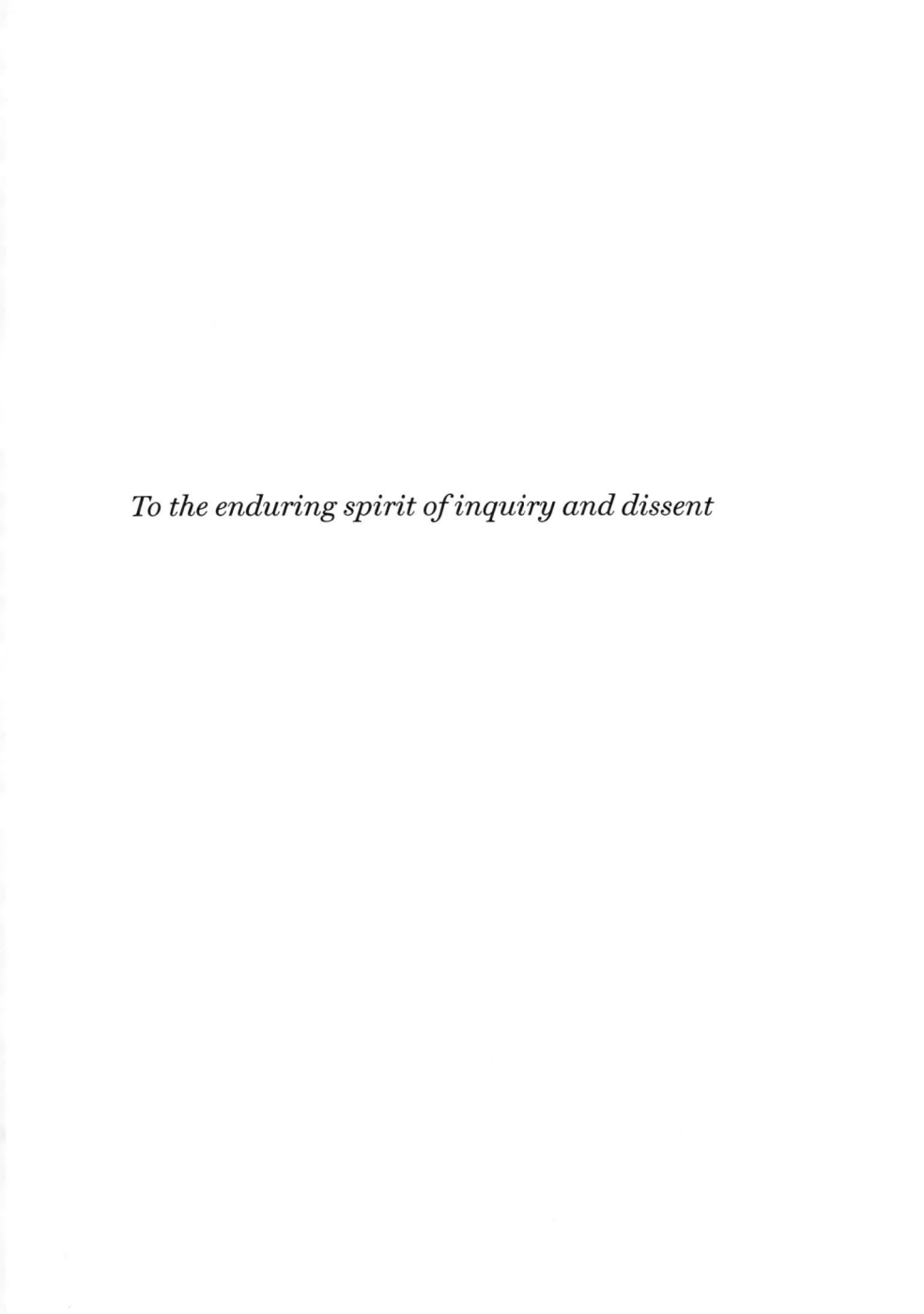

CONTENTS

Preface 2

Introduction 8

Wordsmiths 19

Scholars 79

Maestros 135

Visionaries 173

Innovators 229

Two Concluding Thoughts 282

Notes 286

Index of Thinkers 288

About the Curators 294

About Infinite Books 296

PREFACE

by Vatsal Kaushik

It all started with a tweet from Jim O'Shaughnessy on December 28, 2020:

Two Thoughts from Buckminster Fuller:

There is nothing in a caterpillar that tells you it's going to be a butterfly.

Don't fight forces, use them.

Three years and over 2,000 thoughts later, Jim's Two Thoughts series has become a daily institution.

Curation is a form of storytelling, and, like all great narratives, it offers a glimpse of the storyteller. The Two Thoughts series, mirroring Jim's multifaceted life, spans multiple disciplines: science, rationality, art, courage, epistemology, evolution, finance, human nature, and more.

Like this book, Jim contains multitudes. He's the quantitative finance pioneer who is a patron of the arts. He's the Wall Street guru who has been on *Oprah*. He's the leading businessman with multiple bestselling books. He's the baby boomer who embraces transformative technology. Founder, investor, podcast host, writer, loquacious provocateur: the common thread of insatiable curiosity, optimism, and 60+ years of accumulated wisdom is reflected in the curated quotes presented herein.

I'd been working with Jim on the *Infinite Loops* podcast[1] for about a year when I noticed that his daily doses of wisdom had started to grow a following of their own.

With just one tweet a day, the force of compounding was busy at work—and I wanted to use it:

> *Would totally sign up for a @jposhaughnessy daily quotes newsletter.* —ANNA GAT, FOUNDER OF INTERINTELLECT

> *Mmm 🅐 I love waking up to Two Thoughts with J.O. Should compile these into a short book or desk calendar.* —SARAH KATILYN, INVESTOR

Anna's suggestion gave birth to the *Infinite Loops* newsletter[2] in January 2022. This was an improvement, but it wasn't the endgame.

As Marshall McLuhan once famously said, "The medium is the message." Timeless wisdom deserves a medium more robust and permanent than Twitter/X or emails, and thus a book, tangible and enduring, became Two Thoughts' natural destination.

I often skip prefaces that try to tell me how to read the book, and by all means, you do you! But, if you would humor me with one suggestion to make your experience far more meaningful, I'd say try not to read it cover to cover.

Imagine you're visiting New York or Paris, a historic and vibrant city brimming with hidden alleys, bustling markets, and serene parks. To try to see it all in one frenzied day would be a waste, catching only the briefest glimpses of its essence. Rather, it's the leisurely strolls through its streets, the unhurried coffees in quaint cafes, and the unexpected conversations with locals that truly bring a city's story to life. Each return to this urban tapestry, much like revisiting chapters in a book, allows you to uncover new secrets and savor familiar joys, enriching your understanding and appreciation of its many layers.

Along with each set of Two Thoughts, you will find a few lines about the thinkers who gave them to us. Some names you'll be seeing for the first time, while some may be as familiar to you as a childhood friend. Some will be people you respect immensely. Others...not so much. Have a conversation with these people, contest their ideas, take inspiration, but never value the thought based on the weight of the thinker's name. As Eleanor Roosevelt once said, "Great minds discuss ideas; average minds discuss events; small minds discuss people."

Except...she never said it.[3] The quote is widely misattributed to Eleanor, and that's okay! Quotes, like memes, have a curious habit of escaping the clutches of their originator, entering the culture, and being remixed, reworked, and reattributed. Their true origin is often a mystery.

When we have detected a misattributed Two Thought, we have addressed it in the notes instead of removing it, for the real value of this book is not in what is said and even less in who said it, but in what you do with it. Make these quotes your own!

I once asked Jim if he had any favorite quotes he wanted to feature in the book. His response: "For me, it's the synthesis that comes out of contemplating them that I find interesting." That's what I ask of you. Contemplate, scribble in the margins, go on tangents, find weird relationships between these quotes (and yes, some of them will contradict each other). Use it not only as a book of thought, but as a book of action.

The *Two Thoughts* curation has experienced its own metamorphosis. Open to any random page, and the quote on it has likely been transported from a scribbling in one of Jim's handwritten journals, to his Twitter, to our newsletter, and now to this book. Along the way, it has been touched, read, considered, remixed, and even rejected by countless people, each individual interaction the possible catalyst for an explosion of original thought and, of course, original action.

My colleagues Ed William, Dylan O'Sullivan, Michaël "Liberty" Graham Richard, and the entire team at O'Shaughnessy Ventures have contributed to selecting the quotes, writing the Thinker introductions, proofreading, editing, and countless other tasks involved in bringing a book to life. But of course, *Two Thoughts* wouldn't be a thing if not for Jim O'Shaughnessy. It is he who spotted this caterpillar out in the wild and nurtured it into a butterfly.

INTRODUCTION

"We say 'seeing is believing,' but actually, as Santayana pointed out, we are all much better at believing than at seeing. In fact, we are seeing what we believe nearly all the time and only occasionally seeing what we can't believe."

—Robert Anton Wilson

"If people want happiness so badly, why don't they attempt to understand their false beliefs? First, because it never occurs to them to see them as false or even as beliefs. They see them as facts and reality, so deeply have they been programmed."

—Tony de Mello

We humans are an interesting lot.

We confuse our opinions and beliefs with statements of fact, infuse them with emotions, then adopt them as extensions of our sense of self. It's a tendency that, rather conveniently for the ego, reframes the very *concept* of pushback as a personal attack.

In his book *Prometheus Rising*, Robert Anton Wilson cites the work of Leonard Orr, who divides the human mind into two characters: the Thinker and the Prover.

Orr puts forward that the Thinker can entertain all manner of thoughts, often taking cues from the collective wisdom of family and friends, movies and books, religions and philosophies, before conflating them with its own (often unconsciously).

In other words, the Thinker can imagine anything and everything under the sun, no matter how fantastical or illogical. Magic or mundane, we give it free rein to "believe as many as six impossible things before breakfast," as the Queen says to Alice in *Through the Looking Glass*.

The Thinker also possesses the ability to shade our world in any way it desires.

It can envision life as a kaleidoscopic journey, filled with weird and wonderful friends and strangers, or a dark walk through mean streets, overshadowed by an unfeeling, unjust universe, forever "out to get" it.

It can declare baseball as the national pastime or proclaim football as the rightful heir to that throne. It can envision Milton Friedman's free markets as the only solution, or Karl Marx's proclamations as the one true doctrine.

The point is, after much or little thought, the Thinker *decides* that something is right or wrong, true or false—and, upon doing so, shuts off.

Then the Prover takes the wheel!

The Prover's job is simple. It looks at these instinctual beliefs and then—you guessed it—gets to work on proving them. Do you believe that your hometown team is an extension of you? The Prover will make it so. Are you Team Red or Team Blue? Doesn't matter. Whichever you are, the Prover will provide a steady flow of information to both corroborate and concretize what the Thinker has preordained.

The Prover doesn't *know* how much or how little effort the Thinker gave to forming these beliefs. Its job is simple: to prove what you believe is true.

If the Prover is good at its job, you will elevate these beliefs to "hills you could die on." Yet, because its job is to prove rather than question, the Prover is prone to shut down thoughts like *What if I'm wrong?* And remember: things that go unquestioned go unseen.

The phrase "seeing is believing" is precisely backward: believing is seeing. This is the case with *all* of us, for it comes fully preinstalled with HumanOS—an app that runs ceaselessly and silently in the background of our minds.

Why is being aware of this software "glitch" in our HumanOS useful? Well, I believe that getting to know your Thinker and Prover can not only help you better understand the thoughts and actions of those around you, but unlock a deeper understanding of yourself.

When people marry their beliefs about *things* to their rawest *emotions* and deepest *desires*—a marriage that only grows stronger over time—their Prover kicks into overdrive to validate said beliefs so conclusively that no number of arguments or facts will be able to pierce their "reality tunnel."

To see the truth of this, simply peruse social media on any given day, where, to paraphrase Rudyard Kipling, we humans behave as islands of contrary beliefs, shouting at each other over seas of misunderstanding.

Another dangerous (sometimes deadly) outcome of this process is that people begin to suffer from "filter failure." Depending on the strength of their now emotionally laden belief, their Prover might firewall so much vital information from their minds that they become, in an intellectual sense, braindead. If you find this hard to *believe*, look no further than our rich history of fundamentalist religions and totalitarian regimes (to expedite the process, start with those you disagree with most).

Each and every belief and belief system that has gained mass acceptance over the years has taken flight when a majority of people's Provers began following the same paths, converging to form a consensus reality—a reality that can be virtuous or vicious, depending on the nature of the beliefs.

Diverging from this mass convergence and falling out of sync with consensus reality can lead to either a very perilous or lucrative position. If you held on to heretical thoughts during the rise of the Spanish Inquisition, you risked execution like Francisca de Carvajal. If you "thought differently" during the rise of Silicon Valley, you risked becoming a billionaire like Steve Jobs.

As a general rule, the more open and free a society is, the greater the impact of people who challenge—or at least question—conventional wisdom.

This wasn't always so, and within many cultures and communities today, it still isn't.

When we study history, we see that, prior to the Computer Age, consensus reality changed very slowly and was largely hostile to anyone who dared to stand behind new ideas.

It's important to remember that untold generations of humankind lived and died under the same consensus reality, often unwilling or unable to even question it, sometimes unaware there was anything to question at all.

With the rise of the internet, however, things have accelerated to the nth degree. Today, no individual is without a microphone, no group without a megaphone. It's a daunting and debilitating situation for many, for the never-ending tsunamis of information are smashing against a neurochemistry that was never designed for such an onslaught—and the results are telling.

Around the world, people are retreating down their own well-worn and ever-narrowing paths, unconsciously turning off their Thinker and sending their Prover in search of subgroups and sameness.

Is this inevitable? I think not.

Is it possible to renovate our reality tunnel, upgrading our systems and strategies to smoke out the invisible ideas living rent-free in our heads?

I think so.

There's no magic to it—nothing but our willingness to take on the endless and uncomfortable task of questioning our surroundings, questioning ourselves: thinking, proving, then thinking again.

Which brings us to *Two Thoughts*.

This is not a book for Thinkers *or* Provers, but for those endeavoring to explore the terra incognita between the two; those wanting, as Robert Anton Wilson did, to navigate those deep and choppy waters between seeing and believing.

In the pages that follow, you will be cast in the dual role of Thinker *and* Prover, rubbing shoulders with some of the greatest minds from the worlds of business and art, science and philosophy, and more. Do not let their greatness persuade or intimidate you, however. Remember: their thoughts are not gospel, but merely good-faith investigations of consensus reality. Confront their contributions for what they are: thoughts that require proving, proofs that require thinking; slices of reality to be held up to the light and weighed but never worshiped, entertained but never exalted, and chewed over but never swallowed whole.

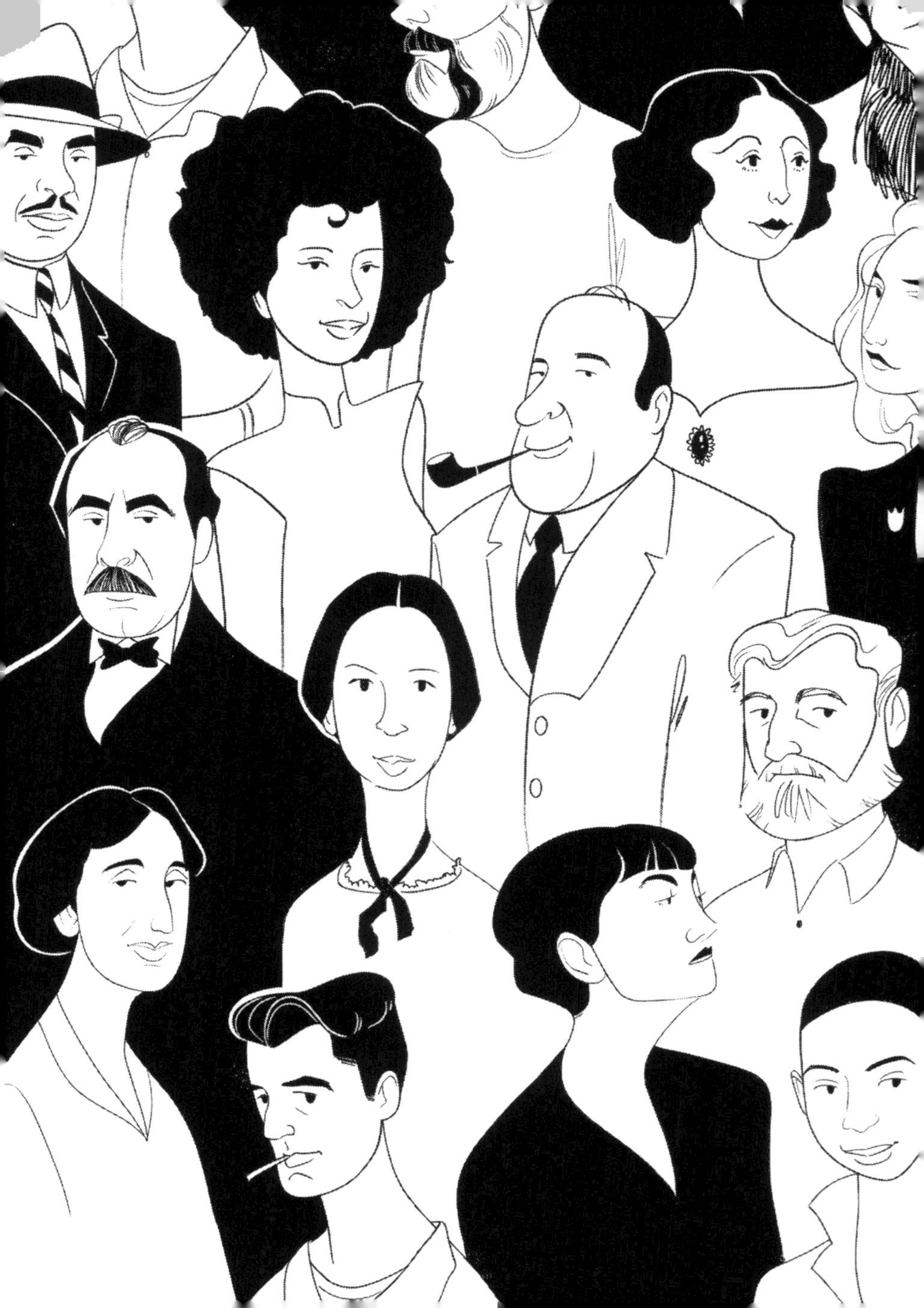

WORDSMITHS

writers, playwrights, poets,
satirists, cartoonists

Two Thoughts from
DAVID FOSTER WALLACE

"Everybody is identical in their secret unspoken belief that way deep down they are different from everyone else."

"You will become way less concerned with what other people think of you when you realize how seldom they do."[4]

David Foster Wallace was an American author and essayist known for his novel *Infinite Jest* and his collection of essays *A Supposedly Fun Thing I'll Never Do Again.* His writing explored the relationship between self-awareness and depression and the challenges of living in a postmodern world.

Two Thoughts from
DOROTHY PARKER

"The cure for boredom is curiosity. There is no cure for curiosity."[5]

"Of course I talk to myself. I like a good speaker, and I appreciate an intelligent audience."

Dorothy Parker was an American poet and playwright often remembered for her witty and wisecracking style. One of the founders of the Algonquin Round Table, an informal literary group based in New York City, Parker later relocated to Hollywood to pursue screenwriting. Her success there, which included two Academy Award nominations, was curtailed when she was placed on the Hollywood blacklist during the McCarthyism era.

Two Thoughts from

ROBERT A. HEINLEIN

"Progress isn't made by early risers. It's made by lazy men trying to find easier ways to do something."

"Always listen to experts. They'll tell you what can't be done, and why. Then do it."

Robert Heinlein was an American writer and naval officer known as "the dean of science fiction writers." An aeronautical engineer by training, Heinlein was among the first to emphasize scientific accuracy in his fiction, thereby pioneering the subgenre of hard science fiction. For such works as *Starship Troopers* and *Stranger in a Strange Land*, Heinlein was named the first Grand Master of the Science Fiction and Fantasy Writers Association in 1974.

Two Thoughts from

NEIL GAIMAN

"Fairy tales are more than true: not because they tell us that dragons exist, but because they tell us that dragons can be beaten."

"I hope that in this year to come, you make mistakes. Because if you are making mistakes, then you are making new things, trying new things, learning, living, pushing yourself, changing yourself, changing your world. You're doing things you've never done before, and more importantly, you're doing something."

Neil Gaiman is a British author known for his work in fantasy, including novels, comic books, graphic novels, and films. Some of his most notable works include *The Sandman* comic book series, *Stardust*, *American Gods*, *Coraline*, and *The Graveyard Book*, which won the Newbery and Carnegie Medals. Gaiman is also fond of fountain pens and is known to write the first draft of each of his books with one.

Two Thoughts from
CHERYL STRAYED

"You don't have a right to the cards you believe you should have been dealt. You have an obligation to play the hell out of the ones you're holding."

"Fear, to a great extent, is born of a story we tell ourselves."

Cheryl Strayed is an American writer and podcaster. She is best known for her 2012 memoir *Wild: From Lost to Found on the Pacific Crest Trail*. In 2014, *Wild* was adapted into an Academy Award–nominated film of the same name, directed by Jean-Marc Vallée. In addition to her books, Strayed has published essays in the likes of the *New York Times* and *Vogue*. In 2019, as part of the Statues for Equality initiative, Strayed was one of ten women for whom statues were constructed in New York.

Two Thoughts from

KAHLIL GIBRAN

"If you love somebody, let them go, for if they return, they were always yours. If they don't, they never were."

"The smallest act of kindness is worth more than the greatest intention."

Kahlil Gibran was a Lebanese American poet, artist, and philosopher who gained widespread recognition for his thought-provoking work *The Prophet*. Published in 1923, the book remains popular among readers as a collection of philosophical essays in poetic prose. Gibran's extensive body of literature primarily focuses on themes of love, spirituality, and the human condition. He is considered one of the most influential literary figures of the twentieth century, with his timeless wisdom continuing to inspire generations around the world.

Two Thoughts from
ERNEST HEMINGWAY

"There is nothing noble in being superior to your fellow man; true nobility is being superior to your former self."

"The world breaks everyone and afterward many are strong at the broken places."

Ernest Hemingway was an American novelist, short-story writer, and journalist, known for his concise and straightforward writing style. He won the Pulitzer Prize in 1953 for his novel *The Old Man and the Sea* and the Nobel Prize in Literature in 1954. Hemingway's writing often explored themes of masculinity, war, and the human condition.

Two Thoughts from
LEO TOLSTOY

"Everyone thinks of changing the world, but no one thinks of changing himself."

"We can know only that we know nothing. And that is the highest degree of human wisdom."

Leo Tolstoy was a Russian writer and philosopher who is widely regarded as one of the greatest novelists of all time. His most famous works, such as *War and Peace* and *Anna Karenina*, explored themes of love, family, and human nature, often in the context of historical events. Tolstoy was also a prominent thinker and activist, advocating for nonviolence and social justice.

Two Thoughts from
JOHN IRVING

"If you don't feel that you are possibly on the edge of humiliating yourself, of losing control of the whole thing, then probably what you are doing isn't very vital."

"It is hard work and great art to make life not so serious."

John Irving is an American Canadian author and screenwriter perhaps best known for his coming-of-age novel *The World According to Garp*. In 2000, Irving received an Academy Award for his cinematic adaptation of his eponymous novel *The Cider House Rules*. To date, four of Irving's novels have reached #1 on the *New York Times* bestseller list.

Two Thoughts from

ANTHONY BURGESS

"When a man cannot choose, he ceases to be a man."

"To be left alone is the most precious thing one can ask of the modern world."

Anthony Burgess was an English writer and composer best known for his dystopian satire *A Clockwork Orange*. In 1971, the novel was adapted into a controversial film by Stanley Kubrick, which remains a cult classic to this day. In addition to being a writer, Burgess was an accomplished composer, releasing more than 250 musical works over the course of his life.

Two Thoughts from

ALICE WALKER

"The most common way people give up their power is by thinking they don't have any."

"What the mind doesn't understand, it worships or fears."

Alice Walker is an American novelist, poet, and social activist, best known for her Pulitzer Prize–winning novel *The Color Purple*. Alongside her literary accomplishments, Walker has also been actively involved in civil rights and women's rights movements throughout her life. Her work often deals with themes such as race, gender, and the human spirit.

Two Thoughts from

CARLOS RUIZ ZAFÓN

"Envy is the religion of the mediocre. It comforts them, it soothes their worries, and finally it rots their souls."

"Few things are more deceptive than memories."

Carlos Ruiz Zafón was a Spanish novelist. He is best known for his novel *The Shadow of the Wind*, which has sold upwards of 15 million copies. The author of six novels, Zafón has had his fiction published in over 45 countries and translated into more than 50 languages. From 1994 on, Zafón lived and worked in Los Angeles as a screenwriter.

Two Thoughts from

HEINRICH HEINE

"Wherever they burn books they will also, in the end, burn human beings."

"A brainiac notices everything, an ignoramus comments about everything."

Heinrich Heine was a German poet and critic whose lyrical poetry was set to music by the likes of Franz Schubert. Considered a member of the Young Germany movement, Heine held political views that led to many of his works being banned by German authorities, which only added to his fame. Heine spent his last 25 years as an expatriate in Paris, ultimately being laid to rest in Montmartre Cemetery.

Two Thoughts from

FYODOR DOSTOEVSKY

"Nowadays, almost all capable people are terribly afraid of being ridiculous, and are miserable because of it."

"The cleverest of all, in my opinion, is the man who calls himself a fool at least once a month."

Fyodor Dostoevsky was a Russian novelist, philosopher, and journalist. He is considered one of the greatest writers in the history of literature. Dostoevsky's writing, which includes books like *Crime and Punishment* and *The Brothers Karamazov*, is known for its psychological depth and philosophical insights, and his ideas have had a profound impact on literature and thought.

Two Thoughts from

ALDOUS HUXLEY

"One believes things because one has been conditioned to believe them."

"That men do not learn very much from the lessons of history is the most important of all the lessons that history has to teach."

Aldous Huxley was an English writer and philosopher known for his novels, including *Brave New World, Eyeless in Gaza,* and *Island.* He was also a humanist and pacifist who explored the spiritual dimensions of human existence. Huxley was interested in the role of conditioning and indoctrination in shaping human behavior and believed it was essential to question the assumptions and values of one's culture.

Two Thoughts from
TIM KREIDER

"It's easy to demonstrate how progressive and open-minded and loyal you are when it costs you nothing."

"Because the essence of creativity is fucking around; art is that which is done for the hell of it."

Tim Kreider is an American essayist and cartoonist whose work has appeared in the *New York Times*, *Film Quarterly*, and *the Comics Journal*. His comic *The Pain—When Will It End?* ran in the *Baltimore City Paper* for 12 years and was collected in three books by Fantagraphics. Kreider has also published multiple collections of essays, such as *We Learn Nothing* and *I Wrote This Book Because I Love You.*

Two Thoughts from

EMILY DICKINSON

"Forever is composed of nows."

"Truth is so rare, it is delightful to tell it."

Emily Dickinson was an American poet known for her unique writing style and unconventional approach to life. Although she lived a relatively reclusive life, her powerful poems have left an indelible mark on American literature. During her lifetime, she wrote nearly 1,800 poems, but only a few were published. It was not until after her death that her vast body of work, characterized by its insightful exploration of emotions and spirituality, gained widespread recognition and acclaim.

Two Thoughts from
AESCHYLUS

"It is in the character of very few men to honor without envy a friend who has prospered."

"To learn is to be young, however old."

Aeschylus was an ancient Greek tragedian, often cited as the father of the genre. Over the course of his life, Aeschylus wrote over 90 plays, the most famous being *Prometheus Bound*, which tells the myth of Prometheus stealing fire from the gods. According to Aristotle, Aeschylus was the first dramatist to expand the number of characters in the theater and allow conflict between them.

Two Thoughts from
ROBINSON JEFFERS

"I believe that the universe is one being, all its parts are different expressions of the same energy."

"That public men publish falsehoods is nothing new. Be angry at the sun for setting if these things anger you."

Robinson Jeffers was an American poet and playwright whose themes of nature and pantheism cemented him as an icon of the environmental movement. Jeffers skyrocketed to fame with his third book, *Tamar and Other Poems*, which led to him becoming the favorite poet of Charles Bukowski and others. Jeffers's 1947 adaptation of Euripides's *Medea* became a hit Broadway play starring Dame Judith Anderson.

Two Thoughts from

MARGARET FULLER

"Today a reader, tomorrow a leader. If you have knowledge, let others light their candles in it. Very early I knew that the only objective in life was to grow."

"Men for the sake of getting a living forget to live."

Margaret Fuller was an American writer and women's rights advocate who was regarded as a pioneer of the transcendentalist movement in the United States. Fuller was her country's first female war correspondent and full-time book reviewer. Her *Woman in the Nineteenth Century* is considered the first major feminist work in the United States.

Two Thoughts from
ANAÏS NIN

"We don't see things as they are, we see them as we are."[6]

"Life is a process of becoming, a combination of states we have to go through. Where people fail is that they wish to elect a state and remain in it. This is a kind of death."

Anaïs Nin was a French-born American author and essayist who first garnered critical acclaim following the publication of her personal diaries. Over the course of her life, Nin explored a variety of genres and themes, from literary criticism and experimental fiction to erotica and psychoanalysis.

Two Thoughts from

ANTON CHEKHOV

"The world is, of course, nothing but our conception of it."

"Do silly things. Foolishness is a great deal more vital and healthy than our straining and striving after a meaningful life."

Anton Chekhov was a Russian playwright and short-story writer. He is often regarded as one of the three forefathers of early modernism in theater, alongside Henrik Ibsen and August Strindberg. A physician by profession, Chekhov wrote plays that were not well-reviewed by critics at first, but later came to be revered thanks to staged productions by Konstantin Stanislavski's Moscow Art Theatre. To this day, such plays as *The Seagull*, *Uncle Vanya*, *Three Sisters*, and *The Cherry Orchard* are continually staged around the world.

Two Thoughts from

NEIL POSTMAN

"Children enter school as question marks and leave as periods."

"People in distress will sometimes prefer a problem that is familiar to a solution that is not."

Neil Postman was an American author and media theorist. He was famously critical of digital technology. A prolific writer, Postman authored more than 20 books regarding technology and education, including *Amusing Ourselves to Death* and *The End of Education*. In 1959, Postman began teaching at New York University, where he founded a graduate program in media ecology.

Two Thoughts from
KHALED HOSSEINI

"Children aren't coloring books. You do not get to fill them with your favorite colors."

"Reading is an active, imaginative act; it takes work."

Khaled Hosseini is an Afghan American novelist. He is best known for *The Kite Runner*, which spent 101 weeks on the *New York Times* bestseller list. The book's success allowed Hosseini, a former physician, to retire from medicine and write full-time. Outside of writing, Hosseini is a US Goodwill Ambassador to the UNHCR and the founder of the Khaled Hosseini Foundation, a nonprofit that provides humanitarian assistance to the people of Afghanistan.

Two Thoughts from

THOMAS PYNCHON

"If they can get you asking the wrong questions, they don't have to worry about answers."

"The general public has long been divided into two parts: those who think that science can do anything and those who are afraid it will."[7]

Thomas Pynchon is an American novelist and short-story writer. He is best known as the author of *Gravity's Rainbow*, which received the National Book Award for Fiction in 1973. In 2014, Pynchon's novel *Inherent Vice* was adapted into a feature film by Paul Thomas Anderson. Pynchon is notoriously reclusive; only a few photographs of him have ever been published.

Two Thoughts from
PHILIP K. DICK

"Don't try to solve serious matters in the middle of the night."

"The basic tool for the manipulation of reality is the manipulation of words. If you can control the meaning of words, you can control the people who must use them."

Philip K. Dick was an American writer and storyteller whose reality-bending novels would become the first works of science fiction to be canonized by the Library of America. Known for his extraordinary prolificacy, Dick published 44 novels and about 121 short stories over the course of his career. In one particularly productive period, from 1968 to 1969, Dick published both *Do Androids Dream of Electric Sheep?* and *Ubik*, the former of which would bring us the *Blade Runner* franchise and the latter of which would win a Hugo Award.

Two Thoughts from

VIRGINIA WOOLF

"You cannot find peace by avoiding life."[8]

"The eyes of others our prisons; their thoughts our cages."

Virginia Woolf was an influential English writer and one of the foremost members of the literary modernist movement. She authored numerous classic works, such as *Mrs. Dalloway*, *To the Lighthouse*, *Orlando*, and *A Room of One's Own*. Woolf pushed the boundaries of style and narrative and explored themes of gender, class, and individualism in her work. She was a central figure in the Bloomsbury Group, an influential circle of intellectuals and artists in London.

Two Thoughts from

MORGAN HOUSEL

"Money's greatest intrinsic value—and this can't be overstated—is its ability to give you control over your time."

"You're twice as biased as you think you are (four times if you disagree with that statement)."

Morgan Housel is an American writer and venture capitalist whose writing has featured in The Motley Fool and the *Wall Street Journal.* In recognition of his business columns, Housel received two Best in Business Awards from the Society of American Business Editors and Writers, as well as a *New York Times* Sidney Award. In 2020, Housel published *The Psychology of Money*, which has sold over four million copies and has been translated into 53 languages.

Two Thoughts from
SAMUEL BECKETT

"Ever tried. Ever failed. No matter. Try again. Fail again. Fail better."

"The creation of the world did not take place once and for all time, but takes place every day."

Samuel Beckett was an Irish avant-garde writer, dramatist, and poet. He was known for his influential contributions to modernist literature and theater, particularly through his groundbreaking play *Waiting for Godot*. The winner of the 1969 Nobel Prize in Literature, Beckett often tackled themes of existentialism, despair, and the absurdity of human existence. He wrote primarily in French before translating his works into English, and his minimalist style has influenced generations of writers and artists.

Two Thoughts from

H. P. LOVECRAFT

"The oldest and strongest emotion of mankind is fear, and the oldest and strongest kind of fear is fear of the unknown."

"Our brains deliberately make us forget things, to prevent insanity."

H. P. Lovecraft was an American writer primarily known for his influential works in horror fiction. He created a unique cosmic horror genre that explored the fear of the unknown and the limits of human understanding. While Lovecraft's works were not as popular during his lifetime, his posthumous fame has made him one of the most significant authors in the genre with books like *The Call of Cthulhu*, *The Dunwich Horror*, *At the Mountains of Madness*, and more.

Two Thoughts from
SALMAN RUSHDIE

"From the beginning men used God to justify the unjustifiable."

"'Respect for religion' has become a code phrase meaning 'fear of religion.' Religions, like all other ideas, deserve criticism, satire, and, yes, our fearless disrespect."

Salman Rushdie is an Indian-born British American novelist known for his unique blend of historical and magical realism. Following the publication of his fourth novel, *The Satanic Verses*, Rushdie would become the subject of regular death threats and several assassination attempts (largely thanks to the issuing of a fatwa by Ruhollah Khomeini, the then supreme leader of Iran). In 2007, Rushdie was knighted for his services to literature.

Two Thoughts from

JOHN STEINBECK

"No one wants advice—only corroboration."

"A sad soul can kill you quicker, far quicker, than a germ."

John Steinbeck was an American novelist whose works of epic realism cast light on the socioeconomic realities of the twentieth century. Publishing upwards of 30 books over the course of his life, Steinbeck is best known for *East of Eden* and *The Grapes of Wrath*, the latter of which would receive the Pulitzer Prize for Fiction. In 1962, Steinbeck was awarded the Nobel Prize for Literature.

Two Thoughts from

GAYL JONES

"I learned to write by listening to people talk. I still feel that the best of my writing comes from having heard rather than having read."

"Everything said in the beginning must be said better than in the beginning."

Gayl Jones is an acclaimed American novelist, poet, and playwright. She is known for telling rich, powerful stories that delve into the lives of Black Americans. Jones's writing style is heavily influenced by oral traditions, frequently incorporating the distinct rhythms and dialects she encountered when growing up in Kentucky. Her notable works include the novels *Corregidora*, *Eva's Man*, and *The Healing*. In 2022, Jones was honored for lifetime achievement at the 43rd annual American Book Awards.

Two Thoughts from

OLIVER GOLDSMITH

"It has been well observed that few are better qualified to give others advice than those who have taken the least of it themselves."

"People seldom improve when they have no other model but themselves to copy."

Oliver Goldsmith was an Anglo-Irish writer and poet, perhaps best known for his novel *The Vicar of Wakefield*. Goldsmith established himself as an essayist with his *The Citizen of the World*, a collection of works satirizing Western society. Keyed in to the literary scene, Goldsmith was a member of the famous "Club," an exclusive clique of nine writers including Samuel Johnson and Edmund Burke.

Two Thoughts from
JACK KEROUAC

"Great things are not accomplished by those who yield to trends and fads and popular opinion."

"Because in the end, you won't remember the time you spent working in the office or mowing your lawn. Climb that goddamn mountain."

Jack Kerouac was an American novelist and poet, best known as a key member of the Beat generation, a literary movement that inspired and influenced counterculture during the 1950s and 1960s. His most famous work, *On the Road*, is a seminal piece of American literature that chronicles his cross-country road trips, friendships, and self-discovery. Kerouac's spontaneous writing style explored spirituality, personal freedom, and nonconformity.

Two Thoughts from
JEAN-PAUL SARTRE

"Life begins on the other side of despair."

"We are our choices."

Jean-Paul Sartre was a French philosopher, playwright, novelist, and political activist who is widely recognized as a leading figure in the existentialist movement. His seminal works, such as *Being and Nothingness* and *No Exit*, explore themes of freedom, responsibility, and the human condition. Sartre was awarded the Nobel Prize in Literature in 1964 but declined the honor, stating that a writer should not become institutionalized.

Two Thoughts from
BILL BRYSON

"There are three stages in scientific discovery. First, people deny that it is true, then they deny that it is important, finally they credit the wrong person."

"99.99 percent of all species that have ever lived are no longer with us."

Bill Bryson is an American British author widely known for his books on travel, science, and the English language. With a sharp sense of humor and an accessible writing style, Bryson's work appeals to a broad audience, making topics like science easily digestible for readers. Among his popular books are *A Short History of Nearly Everything*, which won multiple awards, and *Notes from a Small Island*, a humorous account of his travels around the United Kingdom.

Two Thoughts from

CHARLES BUKOWSKI

"The free soul is rare, but you know it when you see it—basically because you feel good, very good, when you are near or with them."

"You begin saving the world by saving one man at a time; all else is grandiose romanticism or politics."

Charles Bukowski was a German American poet, novelist, and short-story writer known for his raw and gritty portrayal of lower-class life in Los Angeles. Often referred to as the "laureate of American lowlife," Bukowski was influenced by his own experiences on the fringes of society. Despite a difficult upbringing and a contemptuous attitude toward literary institutions, Bukowski managed to publish thousands of poems, hundreds of stories, and six novels during his lifetime, becoming a cult hero in the process.

Two Thoughts from
FRANCISCO DE QUEVEDO

"He who spends time regretting the past loses the present and risks the future."

"In short, not only are things not what they seem, they are not even what they are called!"

Francisco de Quevedo was a prominent Spanish writer and poet of the baroque period, known for his unique literary style and biting satirical works. Born in 1580, Quevedo made significant contributions to both poetry and prose, including picaresque novels, political and social treatises, and religious and philosophical writings. His wit and sharp humor made him a leading figure in Spain's literary Golden Age.

Two Thoughts from
EURIPIDES

"The wisest men follow their own direction. And listen to no prophet guiding them. None but the fools believe in oracles, forsaking their own judgment."

"Talk sense to a fool and he calls you foolish."

Euripides was a prominent ancient Greek tragedian known for his contributions to classical literature and drama. Born in the fifth century BC, he is considered one of the three great playwrights of ancient Greece, alongside Aeschylus and Sophocles. His works often exhibit complex character development and question traditional societal norms and values. Euripides is said to have written around 92 plays, with 18 surviving in a substantially complete form, including the renowned pieces *Medea*, *Bacchae*, and *The Trojan Women*.

Two Thoughts from

JENNIFER EGAN

"What he needed was to find 50 more people like him, who had stopped being themselves without realizing it."

"It may be that a crowd at a particular moment of history creates the object to justify its gathering."

Jennifer Egan is an American novelist and short-story writer known for her innovative storytelling techniques and unique approach to character development. She has won numerous awards, including the Pulitzer Prize for Fiction in 2011 for her novel *A Visit from the Goon Squad*. Egan's work often centers around themes of identity, the passage of time, and the effects of technology on human relationships.

Two Thoughts from
SAMUEL JOHNSON

"Curiosity is one of the permanent and certain characteristics of a vigorous intellect."

"The chains of habit are too weak to be felt until they are too strong to be broken."

Samuel Johnson was an English writer, poet, and lexicographer. He made significant contributions to the field of literature and is best known for his influential dictionary, *A Dictionary of the English Language*, which was first published in 1755. As a prominent essayist, moralist, and literary critic, Johnson earned the admiration of his contemporaries, and his works continue to be widely read and appreciated. Today, a painting of Samuel Johnson reading with a confused look on his face is used as a popular reaction meme.

Two Thoughts from
JULIAN BARNES

"History is that certainty produced at the point where the imperfections of memory meet the inadequacies of documentation."

"Mystification is simple; clarity is the hardest thing of all."

Julian Barnes was an English author and critic. He is best known for his novel *The Sense of an Ending*, for which he was awarded the Man Booker Prize. Beginning his career as a literary editor and television critic for the likes of the *New Statesman* and the *Observer*, Barnes turned to fiction in 1980, publishing his debut novel, *Metroland*. For his fiction, Barnes was awarded the Gutenberg Prize and the Jerusalem Prize, as well as being named a Commandeur of L'Ordre des Arts et des Lettres.

Two Thoughts from

HILARY MANTEL

"The reader may ask how to tell fact from fiction. A rough guide: anything that seems particularly unlikely is probably true."

"Insight cannot be taken back. You cannot return to the moment you were in before."

Hilary Mantel was a British author renowned for her historical fiction novels, particularly the *Wolf Hall* trilogy about the rise and fall of Thomas Cromwell. The trilogy earned her two Booker Prizes, making her the first woman and only the third author, after Peter Carey and J. M. Coetzee, to win the literary award twice. Mantel once said that she initially wanted to be a historian before becoming a writer of historical fiction, and she refused to write historical fiction that changed the factual events of the period.

Two Thoughts from
RALPH ELLISON

"Power doesn't have to show off. Power is confident, self-assuring, self-starting and self-stopping, self-warming and self-justifying. When you have it, you know it."

"Had the price of looking been blindness, I would have looked."

Ralph Ellison was an American writer and critic who lectured widely on Black culture, folklore, and creative writing. He was best known for his novel *The Invisible Man*, which won the National Book Award in 1953. Aside from *The Invisible Man*, Ellison published only two more collections of essays in his lifetime: *Shadow and Act* and *Going to the Territory*. His second novel, *Juneteenth*, was published posthumously in 1999.

Two Thoughts from

W. SOMERSET MAUGHAM

"To acquire the habit of reading is to construct for yourself a refuge from almost all the miseries of life."

"It's a funny thing about life; if you refuse to accept anything but the best, you very often get it."

W. Somerset Maugham was an English novelist and playwright known for his clarity of style and contemporary themes. During World War I, Maugham worked for Britain's Secret Intelligence Service: an experience to which Maugham would regularly return throughout his literary career. The Modern Library ranked Maugham's *Of Human Bondage* among the best English-language novels of the twentieth century.

Two Thoughts from

RALPH WALDO EMERSON

"Sow a thought and you reap an action; sow an act and you reap a habit; sow a habit and you reap a character; sow a character and you reap a destiny."

"Do not go where the path may lead, go instead where there is no path and leave a trail."

Ralph Waldo Emerson was an American essayist, lecturer, philosopher, and poet who led the transcendentalist movement in the mid-nineteenth century. As an influential proponent of individualism and self-reliance, Emerson explored the spiritual and intellectual heights of human potential. He is famous for several collections of essays, including *Nature* and *Self-Reliance*, that continue to inspire readers over a century after his death. Emerson also mentored prominent writers such as Henry David Thoreau.

Two Thoughts from
FRANZ KAFKA

"Youth is happy because it has the capacity to see beauty. Anyone who keeps the ability to see beauty never grows old."

"It's only because of their stupidity that they're able to be so sure of themselves."

Franz Kafka was a German-speaking Bohemian writer who is widely considered one of the most important figures in twentieth-century literature. His unique writing style often featured absurd, surreal situations that commented on the struggles and anxieties of the human condition. Best known for works like *The Metamorphosis*, *The Trial*, and *The Castle*, Kafka wrote novels and short stories that primarily center on themes of isolation, personal despair, and bureaucratic oppression. Although Kafka did not enjoy widespread fame during his lifetime, his work later gained recognition for its thought-provoking and introspective nature.

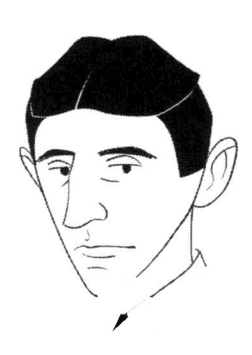

Two Thoughts from

MARGARET WISE BROWN

"We speak naturally but spend all our lives trying to write naturally."

"There seem to be times of reception and times of creation and it is perhaps difficult not to confuse the two."

Margaret Wise Brown was an American author best known for her contributions to children's literature, with classic books like *Goodnight Moon* and *The Runaway Bunny*. Her unique and innovative writing style has captivated generations of young readers since the 1940s. Brown's ability to convey simple, relatable, and timeless stories in a soothing manner has endeared her to children and parents alike.

Two Thoughts from
PICO IYER

"Home lies in the things you carry with you everywhere, and not the things that tie you down."

"It's not our experiences that form us but the ways in which we respond to them."

Pico Iyer is a British novelist and essayist who has written on subjects ranging from the Dalai Lama to the Cuban Revolution. As well as contributing to the likes of *Harper's* and the *New York Times*, Iyer has published 15 books, such as *Video Night in Kathmandu*, which have been translated into 23 languages. Writing aside, Iyer has given four TED talks, which have garnered over 10 million views thus far.

Two Thoughts from

NATASHA PULLEY

"A good number of people listened to, and wrote, music because they liked to hear the sound of mathematics."

"Stop looking at it as an impossible thing and start looking at it as a thing that must be done."

Natasha Pulley is a British writer and professor whose fiction explores the borders of magical realism and alternative history. Pulley received a Betty Trask Award for her debut novel, *The Watchmaker of Filigree Street*, which was a *Sunday Times* bestseller in 2016. Her second novel, *The Bedlam Stacks*, was short-listed for the Encore Award.

Two Thoughts from

ALBERTO MORAVIA

"When you aren't sincere you need to pretend, and by pretending you end up believing yourself; that's the basic principle of every faith."

"The less one notices happiness, the greater it is."

Alberto Moravia was an Italian novelist and journalist whose works explored themes of modern sexuality and alienation. His antifascist novel *The Conformist* was adapted into an Academy Award–nominated film by Bernardo Bertolucci in 1970. Moravia was president of PEN International, the worldwide association of writers, between 1959 and 1962.

Two Thoughts from
J. R. R. TOLKIEN

"A man that flies from his fear may find that he has only taken a shortcut to meet it."

"The wide world is all about you: you can fence yourselves in, but you cannot forever fence it out."

J. R. R. Tolkien was an English writer, poet, philologist, and university professor best known for his high-fantasy novels *The Hobbit* and *The Lord of the Rings*. Born in 1892, Tolkien served in the British Army during WWI and went on to become a professor at Oxford University. He drew inspiration from mythology, religion, and his love of linguistics to create highly detailed, complex worlds complete with intricate invented languages.

Two Thoughts from
ROBERT E. HOWARD

"I know this: if life is illusion, then I am no less an illusion, and being thus, the illusion is real to me. I live, I burn with life, I love, I slay, and am content."

"One man's bane is another's bliss."

Robert E. Howard was an American writer of pulp fiction. He is best known for creating the character of Conan the Barbarian and pioneering the sword and sorcery subgenre. Despite dying by suicide at the age of 30, Howard was an incredibly prolific writer and remains one of the best-selling fantasy writers of all time. A number of Howard's stories have been adapted for the screen, most notably *Conan the Barbarian* and *Conan the Destroyer*, both starring Arnold Schwarzenegger.

Two Thoughts from
DONNA TARTT

"I had the epiphany that laughter was light, and light was laughter, and that this was the secret of the universe."

"Forgive me, for all the things I did but mostly for the ones that I did not."

Donna Tartt is an American novelist and essayist who is best known for her novel *The Goldfinch*, which received the Pulitzer Prize for Fiction. In 2019, *The Goldfinch* was adapted into an eponymous feature film written by Peter Straughan and directed by John Crowley. In 2014, Tartt was included in *Time* magazine's "100 Most Influential People" list.

Two Thoughts from
C. S. LEWIS

"The truth is, of course, that what one regards as interruptions are precisely one's life."

"We are what we believe we are."

C. S. Lewis was a British novelist, essayist, and Christian apologist best known for his beloved *Chronicles of Narnia* series, which has sold over 100 million copies worldwide. A prolific writer and scholar, Lewis was also known for his work in literary criticism and his theological writings, including *Mere Christianity* and *The Problem of Pain*. Lewis was a close friend of author J. R. R. Tolkien, and both were members of the informal writing group known as the Inklings. Lewis's career spanned both academia and literature, and his works continue to engage readers to this day.

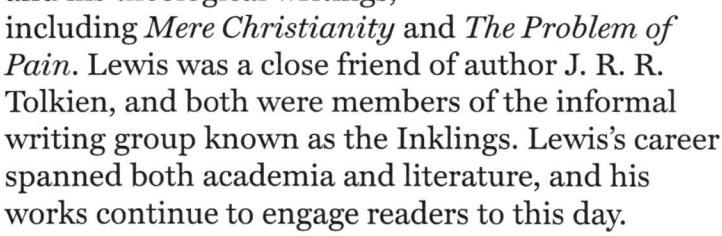

Two Thoughts from
STENDHAL

"All religions are founded on the fear of the many and the cleverness of the few."

"If you think of paying court to those in power, your eternal ruin is assured."

Stendhal was a French writer best known for his novels *The Red and the Black* and *The Charterhouse of Parma*. Though largely unappreciated in the French literary scene of his day, Stendhal has since become celebrated as one of the godfathers of literary realism. Stendhal syndrome, a psychosomatic disorder experienced in close proximity to objects of great beauty, was named after a passage of his writing that described the cultural richness of Florence.

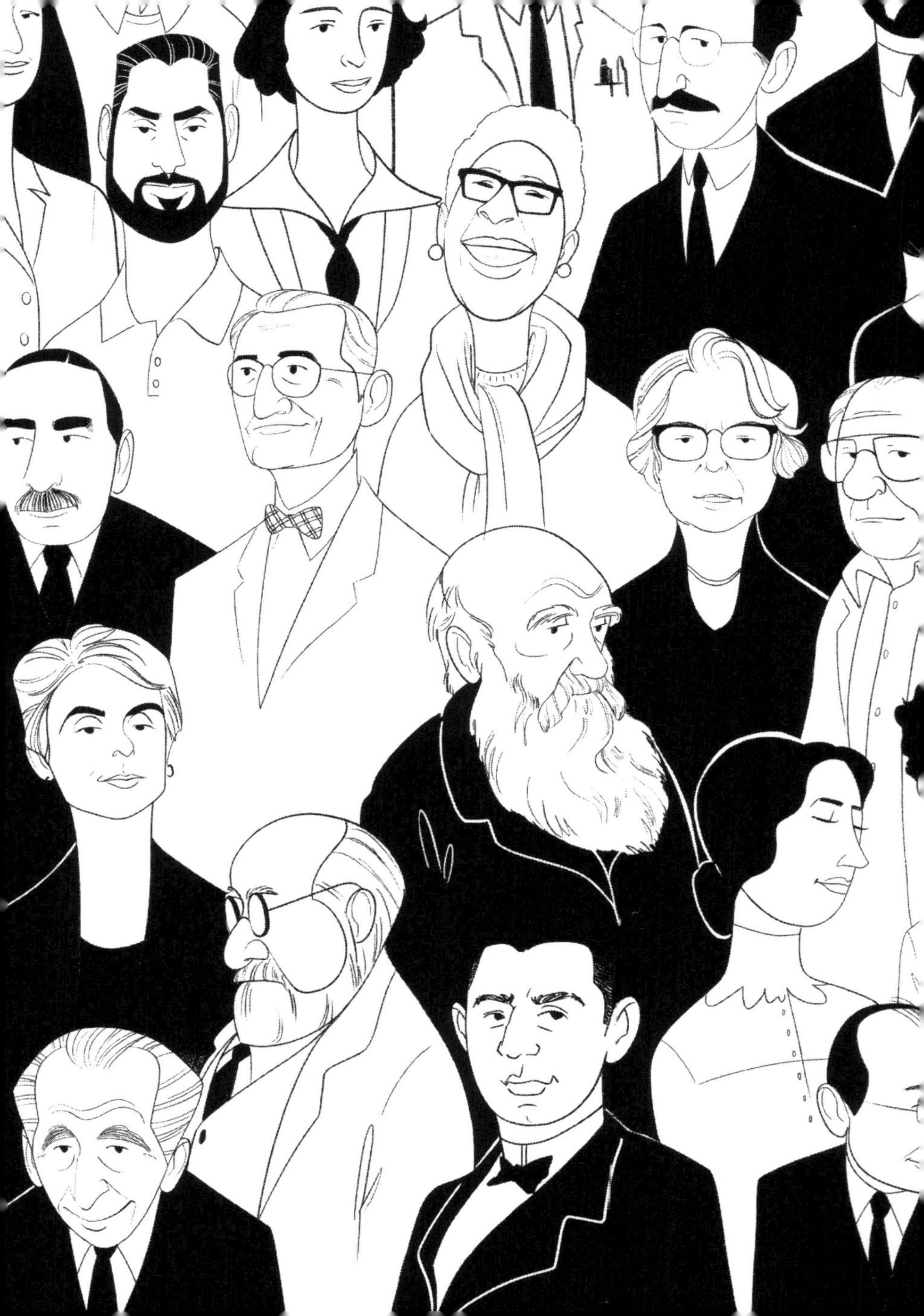

SCHOLARS

researchers, psychologists,
economists, academics, executives

Two Thoughts from
HELEN KELLER

"When one door of happiness closes, another opens; but often we look so long at the closed door that we do not see the one which has been opened for us."[9]

"Life is either a daring adventure or nothing at all."

Helen Keller was an American author, political activist, and lecturer who overcame significant adversity as she was left deaf and blind following an illness in her infancy. Despite these challenges, with the help of Anne Sullivan, her teacher and companion, Keller learned to communicate and became an inspirational public figure advocating for disability rights, women's suffrage, and social change. In 1904, Keller became the first deafblind person to earn a bachelor of arts degree.

Two Thoughts from

MILTON FRIEDMAN

"Inflation is the one form of taxation that can be imposed without legislation."

"A society that puts equality before freedom will get neither. A society that puts freedom before equality will get a high degree of both."

Milton Friedman was a renowned American economist who played a significant role in shaping the economic policies of the United States in the twentieth century. He was a strong proponent of free-market capitalism and believed in the power of individual freedom to promote economic growth and prosperity. Friedman's ideas have been influential in the fields of economics and political philosophy and continue to be debated to this day.

Two Thoughts from
PAUL EKMAN

"Emotions change how we see the world and how we interpret the actions of others. We do not seek to challenge why we are feeling a particular emotion; instead, we seek to confirm it."

"No important relationship survives if trust is totally lost."

Paul Ekman is an American psychologist and professor emeritus at the University of California. He is best known for his research on the relationship between facial expressions and human emotions. As of 2002, Ekman was ranked the 59th most-cited psychologist of the twentieth century. The popular television series *Lie to Me* was based on Ekman's work.

Two Thoughts from

NELL IRVIN PAINTER

"What we can see depends heavily on what our culture has trained us to look for."

"Image works as particularity, not as generalization. That is how art school changed my thinking about history and how visual art set me free."

Nell Irvin Painter is an American historian known for works on the history of the southern United States during the nineteenth century. Previously the Edwards Professor of American History at Princeton University, Painter has also served as president of both the Organization of American Historians and the Southern Historical Association. In 1986, Painter received a Candace Award from the National Coalition of 100 Black Women.

Two Thoughts from
ROBERT K. MERTON

"Anticipatory plagiarism occurs when someone steals your original idea and publishes it a hundred years before you were born."

"Most institutions demand unqualified faith; but the institution of science makes skepticism a virtue."

Robert K. Merton was an American sociologist widely considered a founding father of the field. His work encompassed criminology, serendipity, and mass communication. In 1994, Merton became the first sociologist to receive a National Medal of Science, granted for his founding of the sociology of science. A talented writer, Merton coined such phrases as "role models" and "self-fulfilling prophecy."

Two Thoughts from ———

ROGER L. MARTIN

"Fundamentally, the conventional thinker prefers to accept the world as it is. The integrative thinker welcomes the challenge of shaping the world for the better."

"Simplification, 80–20 style, leads to more business as usual."

Roger L. Martin is an American author and former dean of the Rotman School of Management. Widely regarded as a leading management thinker, Martin has contributed to the likes of the *Washington Post*, the *Financial Times*, and *Harvard Business Review*, and published multiple books, including *The Opposable Mind* and *The Design of Business*.

Two Thoughts from

VIKTOR FRANKL

"When we are no longer able to change a situation, we are challenged to change ourselves."

"Between stimulus and response there is a space. In that space is our power to choose our response. In our response lies our growth and our freedom."

Viktor Frankl was an Austrian neurologist, psychiatrist, and Holocaust survivor. He is known for his book *Man's Search for Meaning*, which chronicles his experiences in the concentration camps and his development of logotherapy, a form of psychotherapy that emphasizes finding meaning in life. He believed that even in the most extreme situations, individuals have the power to choose their attitude and find meaning in their lives.

Two Thoughts from
BENJAMIN GRAHAM

"To be an investor you must be a believer in a better tomorrow."

"Individuals who cannot master their emotions are ill-suited to profit from the investment process."

Benjamin Graham was an American economist and investor known as the "father of value investing." He was a professor at Columbia Business School and mentored notable investors such as Warren Buffett. Graham's approach to investing focused on traits like the intrinsic value of a company and the margin of safety. He believed in the importance of discipline and rationality in investment decisions.

Two Thoughts from
WADE DAVIS

"The world in which you were born is just one model of reality. Other cultures are not failed attempts, they are unique manifestations of the human spirit."

"The measure of a society is not only what it does but the quality of its aspirations."

Wade Davis is a Canadian anthropologist and ethnobiologist. He is best known for his bestselling book *The Serpent and the Rainbow*, which explored Haitian zombie mythology. Outside of writing, Davis was the creator of the documentary series *Light at the Edge of the World*, which aired in 165 countries on the National Geographic Channel and other stations. Today, Davis is professor of anthropology and the BC Leadership Chair in Cultures and Ecosystems at Risk at the University of British Columbia.

Two Thoughts from
PETER GRAY

"The biggest, most enduring lesson of school is that learning is work, to be avoided when possible."

"Perhaps kids today play on the computer because that is one place where they can play freely, without adult intervention and direction."

Peter Gray, an American psychologist and author, is currently a research professor of psychology at Boston College. Gray is also the author of *Psychology*, a widely used introductory psychology textbook that broke ground as the first to bring a Darwinian perspective to the field. Outside of academia, Gray has authored such bestselling books as *Free to Learn* and writes a popular blog for *Psychology Today* entitled *Freedom to Learn*.

Two Thoughts from

CAMILLE PAGLIA

"My advice, as in everything, is to read widely and think for yourself. We need more dissent and less dogma."

"The earth is littered with the ruins of empires that believed they were eternal."

Camille Paglia is an American cultural critic, writer, and professor of humanities and media studies. She is known for her views on feminism, gender, sexuality, and art. Paglia's work often challenges conventional wisdom and promotes free thought and individualism.

Two Thoughts from

DANIEL KAHNEMAN

"The idea that the future is unpredictable is undermined every day by the ease with which the past is explained."

"We can be blind to the obvious, and we are also blind to our blindness."

Daniel Kahneman was an Israeli American psychologist known for his work in the field of behavioral economics, for which he was awarded the Nobel Memorial Prize in Economic Sciences. He is recognized for his research on the psychology of judgment, decision-making, and the irrationality of human behavior.

Two Thoughts from
CHARLIE MUNGER

"Generally speaking, envy, resentment, revenge and self-pity are disastrous modes of thoughts. Self-pity will not improve the situation."

"Avoid extremely intense ideology because it ruins your mind."

Charlie Munger was an American businessman, investor, and philanthropist. He was best known for his work as the vice chairman of Berkshire Hathaway, where he worked alongside Warren Buffett for decades. Munger was known for his wit and wisdom, and his approach to business and investing emphasized rationality, common sense, and patience.

Two Thoughts from

FRIEDRICH HAYEK

"'Emergencies' have always been the pretext on which the safeguards of individual liberty have eroded."

"From the saintly and single-minded idealist to the fanatic is often but a step."

Friedrich Hayek was an Austrian British economist and philosopher whose work focused on the intersection of economics and social phenomena: a focus that would lead Hayek to winning the Nobel Prize in Economics in 1974. In 2011, when celebrating its hundredth year, *American Economic Review* selected Hayek's "The Use of Knowledge in Society" as among the 20 greatest papers ever published by the journal.

Two Thoughts from

SIR JOHN TEMPLETON

"Self-improvement comes mainly from trying to help others."

"An investor who has all the answers doesn't even understand the questions."

Sir John Templeton was a British American investor, philanthropist, and founder of the Templeton Growth Fund. His investment strategies focused on identifying undervalued stocks in emerging markets, which earned him a reputation as a pioneer in global investing. After retiring from the investment industry, Templeton poured his time and wealth into philanthropy, establishing the Templeton Foundation to support research in science, religion, and spirituality.

Two Thoughts from

RICHARD WRANGHAM

"I believe the transformative moment that gave rise to the genus Homo, one of the great transitions in the history of life, stemmed from the control of fire and the advent of cooked meals."

"We should indeed pin our humanity on cooks."

Richard Wrangham is a British-born biological anthropologist known for his groundbreaking research on the role of cooking in human evolution. He is the Ruth B. Moore Professor of Biological Anthropology (retired) at Harvard University and has published numerous books and articles on this subject. Wrangham is also an expert in primate behavior and has conducted extensive field research on chimpanzees in Uganda.

Two Thoughts from
JACK BOGLE

"Your success in investing will depend in part on your character and guts, and in part on your ability to realize at the height of ebullience and the depth of despair alike that this too shall pass."

"Time is your friend; impulse is your enemy."

Jack Bogle was an American investor and business magnate who not only founded the Vanguard Group, but has been credited as being the "father" of index funds. First published in 1999, Bogle's *Common Sense on Mutual Funds: New Imperatives for the Intelligent Investor* remains a classic within the investing community to this day.

Two Thoughts from

JOHN MAYNARD KEYNES

"It is better to be roughly right than precisely wrong."

"Education: the inculcation of the incomprehensible into the indifferent by the incompetent."

John Maynard Keynes was an English economist and philosopher best known for his economic theories on the causes and effects of unemployment. His writings, most notably *The General Theory of Employment, Interest, and Money*, formed the basis for the school of thought known as Keynesian economics. Reformulated as New Keynesianism, his ideas remain a fundamental framework within mainstream macroeconomics.

Two Thoughts from
TIM WU

"Sometimes the crowd is right; often it is wrong. It remains for science to read the balance."

"That which is good or great makes itself known, no matter how loud the clamor of denial. That which deserves to live—lives."

Tim Wu is a Taiwanese American legal scholar and writer known for coining the phrase "network neutrality." As well as writing for the likes of *Slate* and the *New York Times*, Wu authored *The Master Switch*, which was named among the best books of 2010 by the *New Yorker*, *Fortune*, and numerous others. Writing aside, Wu also served on the National Economic Council in the Obama administration and as an advisor to the Biden administration.

Two Thoughts from
DAVID LANDES

"If the gains from trade in commodities are substantial, they are small compared to trade in ideas."

"Scepticism and refusal of authority is at the heart of scientific endeavour. Scientific knowledge dictates economic possibilities."

David Landes was an American professor of economics and history. He is best known for his book *The Wealth and Poverty of Nations*. A childhood prodigy, Landes skipped four grades on his way to receiving a BA from City College of New York and a PhD from Harvard University. A student of cryptanalysis, Landes served in the Signal Corps, deciphering Japanese communications during World War II.

Two Thoughts from

RAYMOND CATTELL

"Plato compared the intellect to a charioteer guiding the powerful horses of the passions, i.e., he gave it both the power of perception and the power of control."

"A society dies if it exceeds a certain degree of individual selfishness."

Raymond Cattell was a British American psychologist widely considered a pioneer in the study of personality. A prolific writer, Cattell authored or contributed to over 500 academic papers over his career and published over 30 standardized psychometric tests. Cattell was the first to propose a hierarchical model of personality, which laid the foundations for the current Big Five (FFM) paradigm.

Two Thoughts from

THOMAS SZASZ

"In the animal kingdom, the rule is, eat or be eaten; in the human kingdom, define or be defined."

"Clear thinking requires courage rather than intelligence."

Thomas Szasz was a Hungarian American psychiatrist and academic. His writings questioned psychiatry's scientific and moral foundations, despite him being a lifetime fellow of the American Psychiatric Association. Throughout his career, Szasz maintained that his stance was not antipsychiatry per se, but anticoercion: in *The Myth of Mental Illness*, he criticized the rise of social control and scientism in the field of medicine.

Two Thoughts from

LUDWIG VON MISES

"Many who are self-taught far excel the doctors, masters, and bachelors of the most renowned universities."

"In a battle between force and an idea, the latter always prevails."

Ludwig von Mises was an Austrian economist and historian, and is considered to be one of the founding fathers of libertarian thought. A mentor of Friedrich Hayek, Mises was a staunch defender of the free market, and consequently a fierce opponent of twentieth-century socialism. In addition to his books, his legacy lives on via the Mises Institute, a libertarian nonprofit headquartered in Auburn, Alabama.

Two Thoughts from

CHARLES DARWIN

"Ignorance more frequently begets confidence than does knowledge."

"We stopped looking for monsters under our bed when we realized that they were inside us."

Charles Darwin was an English naturalist and biologist whose theory of natural selection would become the foundation of evolutionary biology. First published in his 1859 book *On the Origin of Species*, Darwin's theory of evolution would not reach a broad consensus within the scientific community until almost a century later, largely due to the religious implications of his conclusions.

Two Thoughts from

SIGMUND FREUD

"The weakness of my position does not imply a strengthening of yours."

"It is a predisposition of human nature to consider an unpleasant idea untrue, and then it is easy to find arguments against it."

Sigmund Freud was an Austrian neurologist and the founder of psychoanalysis, a clinical method for treating psychopathology through dialogue between a patient and a psychoanalyst. Though widely debated and controversial, Freud's work has left a lasting impact on psychology. His theories on the unconscious mind, dreams, and repression have shaped modern-day therapy practices and understanding of human behavior. Freud was an avid cigar smoker and often used it to stimulate his thought process.

Two Thoughts from

EDWARD GIBBON

"Every person has two educations, one which he receives from others, and one, more important, which he gives to himself."

"I make it a point never to argue with people for whose opinion I have no respect."

Edward Gibbon was an English politician and historian whose magnum opus, *The History of the Decline and Fall of the Roman Empire*, remains a classic work of historical narrative. Gibbon lived an international life, befriending Voltaire and Diderot in Paris before heading to Rome. Known for his epigrammatic style and wit, Gibbon was credited by Winston Churchill as having a great influence on his speechwriting.

Two Thoughts from
EDWARD GLAESER

"The failures of urban renewal reflect a failure at all levels of government to realize that people, not structures, really determine a city's success."

"An economist's definition of hatred is the willingness to pay a price to inflict harm on others."

Edward Glaeser is an American economist and author currently teaching as the Fred and Eleanor Glimp Professor of Economics at Harvard University. During his tenure, Glaeser has published dozens of papers on urban economics and industrial diversity as well as several critically acclaimed books—most notably, *Triumph of the City*. Glaeser is a senior fellow at the Manhattan Institute and a contributing editor to *City Journal*.

Two Thoughts from

TERENCE MCKENNA

"If you don't have a plan, you become part of somebody else's plan."

"The creative act is a letting down of the net of human imagination into the ocean of chaos on which we are suspended, and the attempt to bring out of it ideas."

Terence McKenna was an American ethnobotanist, mystic, author, and lecturer who focused on the exploration of altered states of consciousness, primarily through the use of natural psychedelic substances. He was a strong advocate of personal empowerment and the responsible use of entheogenic plants. McKenna was also known for his unique theories about time, consciousness, and extraterrestrial life. His work has inspired a generation of psychonauts and cultivators of psychedelic plants.

Two Thoughts from
DALE CARNEGIE

"It isn't what you have or who you are or where you are or what you are doing that makes you happy or unhappy. It is what you think about it."

"Talk to someone about themselves and they'll listen for hours."

Dale Carnegie was an American writer and lecturer known for his self-improvement and interpersonal skills courses. He authored the bestselling book *How to Win Friends and Influence People*, which has sold over 30 million copies and remains a popular guide for personal and professional development. Carnegie's teachings focus on effective communication, building relationships, and developing leadership skills. Despite his modest upbringing, Carnegie was able to successfully establish the Dale Carnegie Training company, which continues to offer courses worldwide today.

Two Thoughts from

JONATHAN HAIDT

"People who devote their lives to studying something often come to believe that the object of their fascination is the key to understanding everything."

"The human mind is a story processor, not a logic processor."

Jonathan Haidt is an American social psychologist who specializes in the psychology of morality and the moral emotions. He is the author of several books, including *The Righteous Mind* and *The Happiness Hypothesis*. He is known for his research on the moral foundations of politics and his advocacy for greater ideological diversity in academia.

Two Thoughts from
YUVAL NOAH HARARI

"There are no gods, no nations, no money and no human rights, except in our collective imagination."

"It is an iron rule of history that what looks inevitable in hindsight was far from obvious at the time."

Yuval Noah Harari is an Israeli historian, philosopher, and author of the best-selling books *Sapiens: A Brief History of Humankind* and *Homo Deus: A Brief History of Tomorrow*. He is known for his sweeping theories on the past, present, and future of humanity. His writing explores the role of collective imagination and belief in shaping the development of our societies.

Two Thoughts from
ZENA HITZ

"The idea that real and serious learning is something practiced only by a small elite is stubborn and hard to displace."

"Intellectual life uncovers a human being who is not reducible to his or her economic, social and political contributions."

Zena Hitz is an American author and tutor at St. John's College in Annapolis, Maryland. Hitz has published multiple books, including *Lost in Thought* and *A Philosopher Looks at the Religious Life*, which explore the intersections of literature, philosophy, and religion. She is also the founder and president of the Catherine Project, a free online educational community for adults.

Two Thoughts from

ABRAHAM MASLOW

"To the man who only has a hammer, everything he encounters begins to look like a nail."

"One can choose to go back toward safety or forward toward growth. Growth must be chosen again and again; fear must be overcome again and again."

Abraham Maslow was an American psychologist who is best known for creating Maslow's hierarchy of needs, a theory of psychological health based on fulfilling innate human needs in priority order. He was a pioneer in the field of positive psychology and contributed significantly to humanistic psychology. Maslow's work has been influential in various fields, such as education, management, and self-help.

Two Thoughts from
HENRY GEORGE

"It is not the business of government to make men virtuous or religious, or to preserve the fool from the consequences of his own folly."

"I ask no one who may read this book to accept my views. I ask him to think for himself."

Henry George was an American political economist and journalist whose writings sparked several reform movements during the Progressive Era. His most famous work, *Progress and Poverty*, proposed a single tax to cover the burden of rent and other amenities and has sold millions of copies worldwide. His work inspired the economic philosophy of Georgism, which states that people should own the value of their labor while society should own the value of the land.

Two Thoughts from
DON TAPSCOTT

"To me, this is not an information age. It's an age of networked intelligence, it's an age of vast promise."

"Your network is your filter."

Don Tapscott is a Canadian business executive and author who specializes in the role of technology in business and society. Coauthored with Anthony D. Williams, Tapscott's 2006 book *Wikinomics* became an international bestseller and has been translated into 20 languages. Today, Tapscott serves as the CEO of the Tapscott Group, as well as the cofounder and executive chairman of the Blockchain Research Institute.

Two Thoughts from

BOOKER T. WASHINGTON

"You can't hold a man down without staying down with him."

"A lie doesn't become truth, wrong doesn't become right, and evil doesn't become good, just because it's accepted by a majority."

Booker T. Washington was an American author and educator who served as an advisor to several presidents of the United States. Emancipated from slavery in 1865, Washington would pursue a life of learning and educational reform, becoming the first president of Tuskegee University. Throughout his life, Washington was regarded as the foremost spokesman for African Americans in the post-Reconstruction South.

Two Thoughts from
PHIL STUTZ

"Real change requires you to change your behavior, not just your attitude."

"We like to think we react to the world as it is, when really we react to a world that exists in our own minds."

Phil Stutz is a renowned psychiatrist and therapist who has worked with some of Hollywood's most elite actors and executives over his 40-year career. He is known for his innovative methods and techniques in helping patients overcome anxiety, depression, and various emotional obstacles. His coauthored self-help book, *The Tools*, became an instant bestseller.

Two Thoughts from

HANS ROSLING

"There's no room for facts when our minds are occupied by fear."

"Here's the paradox: The image of a dangerous world has never been broadcast more effectively than it is now, while the world has never been less violent and more safe."

Hans Rosling was a Swedish physician, academic, statistician, and public speaker best known for his work on global health and data visualization. He cofounded the Gapminder Foundation, which developed the Trendalyzer software that represents data in innovative and engaging ways. Rosling's TED talks on common preconceptions about global issues have garnered millions of views.

Two Thoughts from
RAMIT SETHI

"Cynics don't want results; they want an excuse to not take action."

"When you are listening to someone you respect, treat their whispers like screams."

Ramit Sethi is an American personal finance advisor, entrepreneur, and bestselling author, best known for his book *I Will Teach You to Be Rich*. A Stanford University graduate, Sethi has an unconventional approach to financial success that has garnered him a vast following. He has been featured in numerous major publications and television shows, including the *Wall Street Journal*, the *New York Times*, and *The Today Show*.

Two Thoughts from
BENJAMIN P. HARDY

"Wherever your mind goes, your body follows. Wherever your thoughts go, your life follows."

"Few people intentionally define and shape their identity, based on who they plan to be, and then become that person."

Benjamin P. Hardy is an American organizational psychologist, successful entrepreneur, and bestselling author of *Willpower Doesn't Work* and *Personality Isn't Permanent*. As a motivational speaker, Hardy has inspired countless individuals to break free from limiting beliefs and reshape their futures through intentional action and mindset shifts.

Two Thoughts from

JOHN KENNETH GALBRAITH

"The conventional view serves to protect us from the painful job of thinking."

"One of the greatest pieces of economic wisdom is to know what you do not know."

John Kenneth Galbraith was a Canadian American economist, author, and diplomat who contributed greatly to the development of modern economic thought. A longtime Harvard University faculty member, Galbraith served as US ambassador to India during the Kennedy administration and advised several US presidents. He was also a prolific writer who authored over 50 books including his most famous work, *The Affluent Society*, which examined the consequences of overconsumption on society.

Two Thoughts from

ROBERT FRITZ

"If you limit your choice only to what seems possible or reasonable, you disconnect yourself from what you truly want, and all that is left is a compromise."

"The human spirit will not invest itself in a compromise."

Robert Fritz is an American author, management consultant, and composer best known for his work on structural dynamics and the creative process. His foundational book *The Path of Least Resistance* has helped countless individuals and organizations create desired change and tackle challenges in their personal and professional lives.

Two Thoughts from
SUSANNE LANGER

"The high intellectual value of images, however, lies in the fact that they usually, and perhaps always, fit more than one actual experience."

"Music is our myth of the inner life...a laboratory for feeling and time."

Susanne Langer was an American philosopher and educator whose work focused on the intersection of art and mind. Langer is best known for her book *Philosophy in a New Key* and its sequel, *Feeling and Form*. The first American woman to be recognized professionally as a philosopher, Langer was elected a fellow of the American Academy of Arts and Sciences in 1960.

Two Thoughts from

EDWARD SLINGERLAND

"Humans transform the world through our creative technologies, and we cannot survive without them."

"People who are in wu-wei have de, typically translated as 'virtue,' 'power,' or 'charismatic power.' De is radiance that others can detect."

Edward Slingerland is Distinguished University Scholar and Professor of Philosophy at the University of British Columbia. Slingerland is best known for his books *Trying Not to Try*, which explores the concept of wu-wei (effortless action), and *Drunk*, which investigates humanity's relationship with alcohol. His interdisciplinary approach combines ancient Chinese wisdom with modern psychological and cognitive research to better understand human behavior, decision-making, and well-being.

Two Thoughts from ───────────
JAMES GLEICK

"When information is cheap, attention becomes expensive."

"You don't see something until you have the right metaphor to let you perceive it."

James Gleick is an American historian of science whose work centers around the rise and role of technology across society. Thus far, Gleick's two international bestsellers are *Chaos: Making a New Science* and *The Information: A History, a Theory, a Flood*. In 2017, Gleick was elected president of the Authors Guild.

Two Thoughts from
SARAH VOWELL

"The only thing more dangerous than an idea is a belief. And by dangerous I don't mean thought-provoking. I mean: might get people killed."

"Assassins and presidents invite the same basic question: Just who do you think you are?"

Sarah Vowell is an American historian, author, and social commentator known for her witty and insightful writing on American history and culture. She has authored several books, including *Assassination Vacation*, in which she visits historic sites linked to presidential assassinations. Vowell is also known for lending her distinct voice to the character Violet Parr in the animated film *The Incredibles* and its sequels.

Two Thoughts from
ETHAN KROSS

"When supporting others, we need to offer the comfort of Kirk and the intellect of Spock."

"Engage in mental time travel. Another way to gain distance and broaden your perspective is to think about how you'll feel a month, a year, or even longer from now."

Ethan Kross is an American psychologist who specializes in the regulation of emotions. Kross is a professor of psychology at the University of Michigan, where he also serves as the director of the Emotion & Self Control Lab. Outside of academia, Kross is the author of *Chatter: The Voice in Our Head and How to Harness It*, and his research has been featured in the *New York Times* and the *Wall Street Journal*, among others.

Two Thoughts from

YOCHAI BENKLER

"Imperfection is a core dimension of freedom."

"Information, knowledge, and culture are central to human freedom and human development."

Yochai Benkler is an Israeli American author and professor currently serving as the codirector of the Berkman Klein Center for Internet & Society at Harvard University. Within academia, Benkler is best known for coining the phrase "commons-based peer production," as well as for authoring such books as *The Wealth of Networks* and *Network Propaganda*, a body of work for which Benkler received a McGannon Book Award. In 2012, Benkler received a lifetime achievement award from Oxford University.

Two Thoughts from
AJAY AGRAWAL

"We are narrow thinkers, we are noisy thinkers, and it is very easy to improve upon us."

"The new wave of artificial intelligence does not actually bring us intelligence but instead a critical component of intelligence—prediction."

Ajay Agrawal is a Canadian economist, entrepreneur, and professor at the University of Toronto's Rotman School of Management. He is the founder of the Creative Destruction Lab, which has facilitated the growth of numerous successful technology startups. Agrawal is known for his expertise in artificial intelligence (AI) and its economic implications. He has also coauthored books such as *Prediction Machines*, which explores the impact of AI on business and society.

Two Thoughts from
LYNN HUNT

"Human rights are difficult to pin down because their definition, indeed their very existence, depends on emotions as much as on reason."

"Great things sometimes come from rewriting under pressure."

Lynn Hunt is an American historian and author. She specializes in the French Revolution along with intellectual, cultural, and gender history. She served as president of the American Historical Association in 2002 and was given the honor of Distinguished Research Professor at UCLA. Hunt is known for connecting the history of emotions with political and social phenomena, which she discusses in her influential work *Inventing Human Rights*.

Two Thoughts from
KURT LEWIN

"If you want truly to understand something, try to change it."

"When we are young we are like a flowing river—and then we freeze."

Kurt Lewin was a German American psychologist. He is regarded as one of the pioneers of social and applied psychology in the United States. Lewin is best known for his field theory of behavior, which holds that human behavior is a function of an individual's psychological environment. In 2002, a *Review of General Psychology* survey ranked Lewin as the 18th most-cited psychologist of the twentieth century.

Two Thoughts from
TOM PETERS

"If I read a book that cost me $20 and I get one good idea, I've gotten one of the greatest bargains of all time."

"The best leaders, almost without exception and at every level, are master users of stories and symbols."

Tom Peters is an American businessman and writer. He is best known for his book *In Search of Excellence*, which he coauthored with Robert H. Waterman, Jr. Peters served in the US Navy from 1966 to 1970 and made two deployments to Vietnam. In 1981, he moved into the world of business and founded Skunkworks Inc., the Palo Alto Consulting Center, and the Tom Peters Company. Over the course of his writing career, Peters has published upwards of 20 books, written more than 600 syndicated columns, and given over 2,500 speeches.

Two Thoughts from

JEAN BAUDRILLARD

"Nothing is wholly obvious without becoming enigmatic. Reality itself is too obvious to be true."

"We live in a world where there is more and more information, and less and less meaning."

Jean Baudrillard was a French sociologist and philosopher. He is best known for his analyses of media and his formulation of such concepts as hyperreality. Among Baudrillard's most well-known works are *Seduction* and *Simulacra and Simulation*, the latter of which was cited by the Wachowskis as an influence for *The Matrix*. As a professor, Baudrillard began teaching sociology at the Paris X Nanterre before moving to the Université de Paris-IX Dauphine, where he spent the latter part of his academic career.

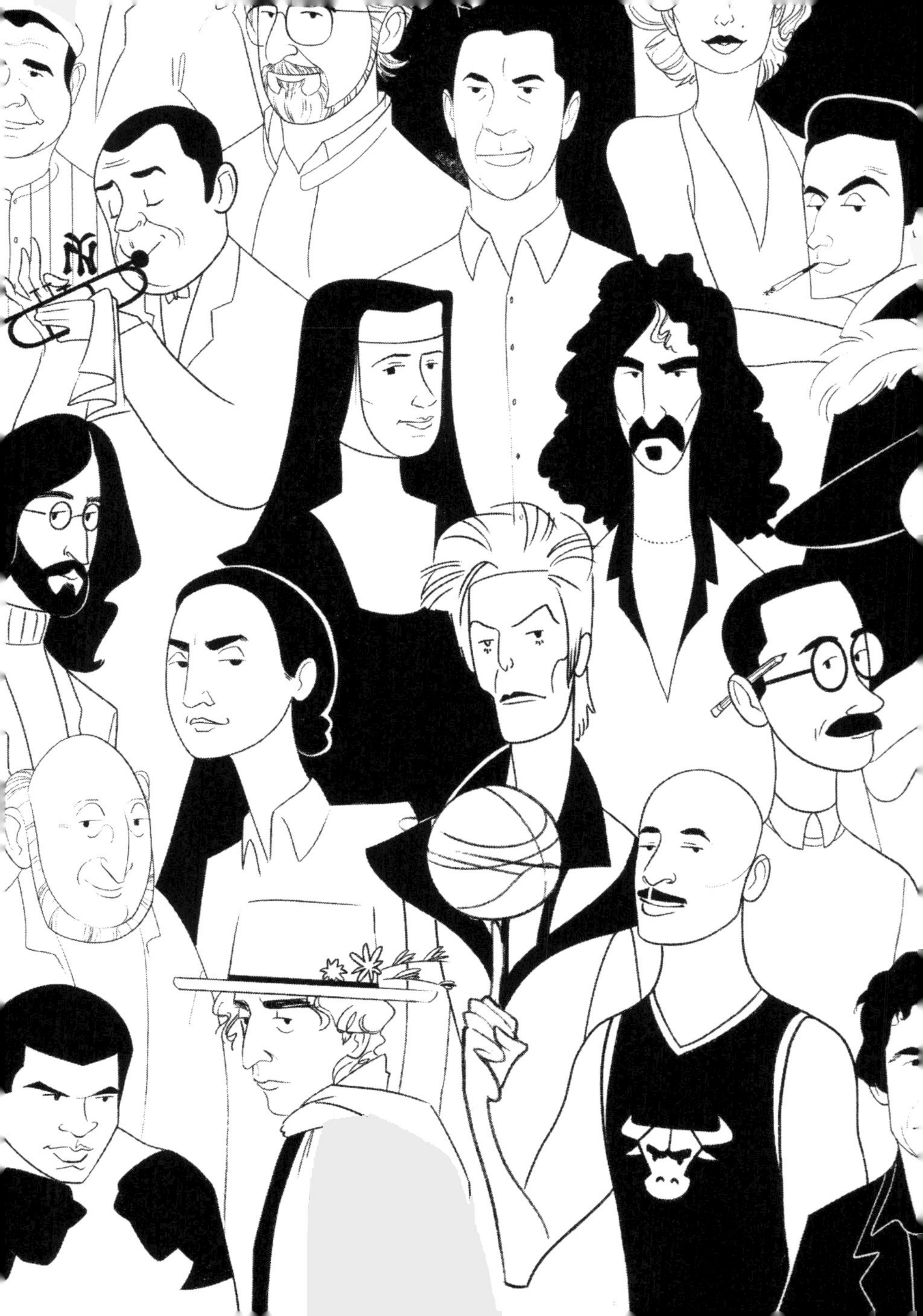

MAESTROS

artists, filmmakers, athletes,
podcasters, entertainers

Two Thoughts from

MUHAMMAD ALI

"I am the greatest. I said that even before I knew I was."

"A man who views the world the same at 50 as he did at 20 has wasted 30 years of his life."

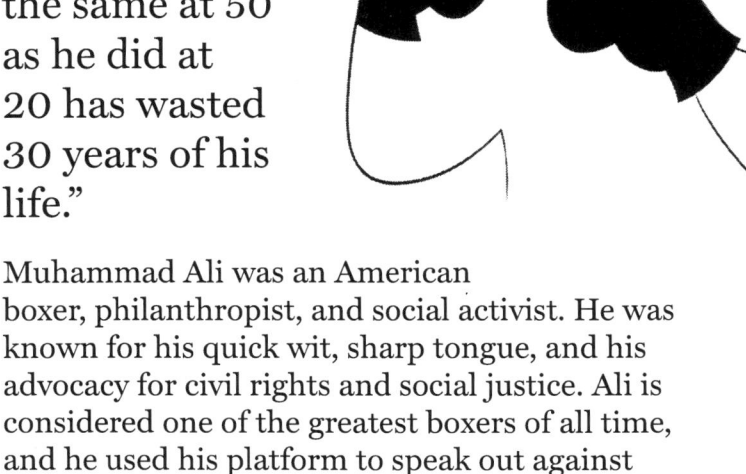

Muhammad Ali was an American boxer, philanthropist, and social activist. He was known for his quick wit, sharp tongue, and his advocacy for civil rights and social justice. Ali is considered one of the greatest boxers of all time, and he used his platform to speak out against racism, injustice, and inequality.

Two Thoughts from
MATTHEW MCCONAUGHEY

"Life is not fair, it never was and it isn't now and it won't ever be. Do not fall into the trap. The entitlement trap, of feeling like you're a victim. You are not."

"Life is a series of commas, not periods."

Matthew McConaughey is an American actor and producer. He began his acting career in the early 1990s and has since become a household name in Hollywood. In addition to his work in film and television, McConaughey is also an author and public speaker, known for his engaging and philosophical perspective on life.

Two Thoughts from

GARRY KASPAROV

"The point of modern propaganda isn't only to misinform or push an agenda. It is to exhaust your critical thinking, to annihilate truth."

"Why settle for thinking like a human if you can be a god."

Garry Kasparov is a Russian chess grandmaster, former World Chess Champion, writer, and political activist. He is widely considered one of the greatest chess players of all time. He is also an outspoken advocate for democracy in Russia and around the world.

Two Thoughts from
BOB DYLAN

"Don't criticize what you can't understand."

"You don't need a weatherman to know which way the wind blows."

Bob Dylan is an American singer-songwriter who is widely regarded as one of the most influential musicians of the twentieth century. His music has been characterized by its poetic lyrics, social and political commentary, and exploration of various genres, including folk, rock, and blues. Dylan has been recognized with numerous awards, including the Nobel Prize in Literature.

Two Thoughts from
GEORGIA O'KEEFFE

"To create one's world in any of the arts takes courage."

"I've been absolutely terrified every moment of my life—and I've never let it keep me from doing a single thing I wanted to do."

Georgia O'Keeffe was an influential American artist renowned for her contributions to modern art, particularly within the genre of precisionism. Born in 1887, O'Keeffe had a career spanning much of the twentieth century, and she became best known for her distinctive paintings of flowers, New York skyscrapers, and New Mexico landscapes. Her art, often interpreted as a statement of feminine expression, played a significant role in the development of American modernism. Over her lifetime, O'Keeffe received numerous accolades, and her works are displayed in major museums around the world. She passed away in 1986, leaving behind a legacy as one of the most significant artists of the twentieth century.

Two Thoughts from
YIP HARBURG

"All the heroes of tomorrow are the heretics of today."

"My heart wants roots. My mind wants wings. I cannot bear their bickerings."

Yip Harburg was an American lyricist and librettist who wrote the lyrics to such standards as "Brother, Can You Spare a Dime?" and "It's Only a Paper Moon." One of Hollywood's leading lyricists, Harburg also wrote all the songs for *The Wizard of Oz*, including "Over the Rainbow." Known for the social commentary of his lyrics, Harburg was an outspoken champion of racial and gender equality, as well as union politics.

Two Thoughts from

ANNIE DUKE

"'I don't know' is not a failure but a necessary step towards enlightenment."

"The more objective we are, the more accurate our beliefs become. And the person who wins bets over the long run is the one with the more accurate beliefs."

Annie Duke is an American former professional poker player, author, and decision strategist. She is known for her success in poker tournaments and her focus on leveraging decision-making skills from the poker table to real-life situations. Following her retirement from the poker world, Duke became an entrepreneur, combining her background in cognitive psychology and poker to create a successful career in corporate consulting and coaching on decision-making processes.

Two Thoughts from
DENZEL WASHINGTON

"I say luck is when an opportunity comes along and you're prepared for it."

"Nothing in life is worthwhile unless you take risks. Fall forward. Every failed experiment is one step closer to success."

Denzel Washington is an American actor, director, and producer. Washington has won numerous awards for his performances on stage and screen, including two Academy Awards, three Golden Globe Awards, and a Tony Award. He is known for his powerful portrayals of complex characters and his commitment to social justice and equality.

Two Thoughts from

STEVEN SPIELBERG

"All of us, every single year, we're a different person. I don't think we're the same person all our lives."

"Why pay a dollar for a bookmark? Why not use the dollar for a bookmark?"

Steven Spielberg is an American director, writer, and three-time Academy Award winner whose films have grossed over $10 billion worldwide so far. Spielberg first became a household name with the release of *Jaws* in 1975. In the decades since, Spielberg has conquered an impressive array of genres, from science fiction (*E.T. the Extra-Terrestrial*) to war (*Saving Private Ryan*) to musicals (*West Side Story*). Spielberg's recurring themes of optimism and innocence have helped him secure a rare combination of commercial success and critical acclaim.

Two Thoughts from ━━━━━━━━
JOE ROGAN

"The time you spend hating on someone robs you of your own time. You are literally hating on yourself and you don't even realize it."

"Reality really is theater. There's no other way to describe it. It's all so nonsensical, ridiculous and chaotic."

Joe Rogan is an American comedian, podcast host, and mixed martial arts commentator who is known for his unfiltered, no-holds-barred style of communication. Through his podcast and comedy, Rogan offers a unique and sometimes controversial perspective on a variety of topics including philosophy, politics, and popular culture. He encourages people to think critically and question the status quo, while also promoting personal growth and self-improvement.

Two Thoughts from
PAUL SIMON

"A man hears what he wants to hear and disregards the rest."

"When I think back on all the crap I learned in high school, it's a wonder I can think at all."

Paul Simon is an American singer-songwriter, best known as one half of folk-rock duo Simon & Garfunkel. For his solo and collaborative work, Simon has garnered 16 Grammy Awards. A two-time inductee into the Rock and Roll Hall of Fame, Simon has been featured on *Rolling Stone*'s lists of both "The 250 Greatest Guitarists of All Time" and the "100 Greatest Songwriters of All Time."

Two Thoughts from

LEONARD COHEN

"Act the way you'd like to be and soon you'll be the way you act."

"Reality is one of the possibilities I cannot afford to ignore."

Leonard Cohen was a Canadian singer-songwriter and poet whose music is renowned for its lyrical depth and minimalistic style. In 1957, Cohen published his first book of poetry, *Let Us Compare Mythologies*, before then turning to music in 1967 with the release of his first studio album, *The Songs of Leonard Cohen*. In 2008, Cohen was inducted into the Rock and Roll Hall of Fame.

Two Thoughts from

MIYAMOTO MUSASHI

"All man are the same except for their belief in their own selves, regardless of what others may think of them."

"Truth is not what you want it to be; it is what it is, and you must bend to its power or live a lie."

Miyamoto Musashi was a Japanese swordsman, philosopher, and writer who is widely regarded as one of the greatest warriors in Japanese history. Musashi's famous book *The Book of Five Rings* is a treatise on strategy, tactics, and martial arts and continues to be studied by martial artists, businesspeople, and politicians to this day. Musashi was undefeated in his 61 duels, fighting his first one at the age of 13.

Two Thoughts from
DAVID BOWIE

"It's always time to question what has become standard and established."

"Tomorrow belongs to those who can hear it coming."

David Bowie was an iconic British singer-songwriter, musician, and actor who significantly impacted the world of music, fashion, and popular culture over his five-decade career. Known for his distinctive voice and constant reinvention of his image, Bowie released classics such as "Space Oddity," "Heroes," and "Life on Mars." In addition to his musical achievements, he also starred in films like *Labyrinth* and *The Man Who Fell to Earth*.

Two Thoughts from
BABE RUTH

"Never let the fear of striking out keep you from playing the game."

"You just can't beat the person who never gives up."

Babe Ruth, born George Herman Ruth Jr., was an American professional baseball player. His power hitting earned him the nickname "the Sultan of Swat." Ruth played 22 seasons in Major League Baseball and set numerous records, including 714 career home runs, a record that stood for 39 years. He was one of the first five players inducted into the Baseball Hall of Fame in 1936. Known for his charismatic personality and larger-than-life attitude, Ruth's presence both on and off the field contributed to the mythos surrounding him.

Two Thoughts from
MARV LEVY

"Age is inevitable. Aging isn't."

"Experience should be a plus as long as it doesn't become complacency. If you say, 'We're not going to change; we didn't do it that way before,' then you've become too old."

Marv Levy is a former American football coach and author who served as a head coach in the NFL for 17 seasons. For his coaching, Levy was inducted into the Pro Football Hall of Fame in 2001 and the Canadian Football Hall of Fame in 2021. Before football, Levy served as a meteorologist at Apalachicola Army Airfield in Florida, but World War II ended before his unit deployed to the Pacific.

Two Thoughts from
JAD ABUMRAD

"There's a Grand Canyon–sized gulf between explanation and experience."

"Continue to reinvent. Keep things moving and changing and growing and always a little bit out of reach."

Jad Abumrad is an American radio host, composer, and producer. He is best known as the founder of the syndicated public radio program *Radiolab* as well as its former host, alongside Latif Nasser and Lulu Miller. In 2011, Abumrad was named a 2011 MacArthur Fellow, with the foundation citing his "engaging audio explorations of scientific and philosophical questions." In 2022, Abumrad announced his retirement from *Radiolab*, joining the faculty at Vanderbilt University.

Two Thoughts from
MAE WEST

"You only live once, but if you do it right, once is enough."

"Between two evils, I always pick the one I never tried before."

Mae West was an American actress, singer, playwright, and screenwriter who pushed the boundaries of societal norms during her career. She was known for her bold and witty humor along with her provocative roles and daring persona. West was charged with "corrupting the morals of youth" for her 1926 play *Sex* and was sentenced to 10 days in prison.

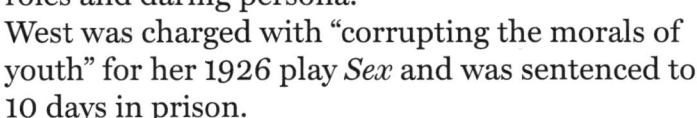

Two Thoughts from
CHRISTOPHER NOLAN

"Breaking rules isn't interesting. It's making up new ones that keeps things exciting."

"You're never going to learn something as profoundly as when it's purely out of curiosity."

Christopher Nolan is a British American filmmaker known for his epic narratives and cinematic use of space-time. Nolan became a household name with films like *The Dark Knight* trilogy, *Inception*, and *Interstellar*. His latest film, *Oppenheimer*, won seven Oscars in 2024, including Best Picture and Best Director. Critical acclaim aside, Nolan has become a household name and has generated a huge amount of box office revenue, with his filmography grossing over $5 billion.

Two Thoughts from
FRANK ZAPPA

"Art is making something out of nothing, and selling it."

"There's a big difference between kneeling down and bending over."

Frank Zappa was an American musician and satirist famous for his artistic and intellectual nonconformity. Emerging on the scene alongside a new generation of improvisatory guitarists such as Jimi Hendrix and Eric Clapton, Zappa would go on to release upwards of 60 albums over the course of his 30-year career. Zappa would also become an accomplished designer, director, and writer, cementing his status as one of the great polymaths of the rock era.

Two Thoughts from
CORITA KENT

"Maybe we are less than our dreams, but that less would make us more than some gods would dream of."

"Consider everything an experiment."

Corita Kent, also known as Sister Mary Corita, was an American Roman Catholic nun, artist, and educator. She became popular for her innovative and vibrant serigraphs, which often incorporated spiritual themes and messages of love and social justice. Her work gained recognition in the 1960s and 1970s, and she would later leave the religious order to fully devote herself to her art. Kent's pieces can be found in various collections around the world, including the Museum of Modern Art in New York and the National Gallery of Art in Washington, D.C.

Two Thoughts from
STEPHEN FRY

"You are who you are when nobody's watching."

"It is the useless things that make life worth living and that make life dangerous too: wine, love, art, beauty. Without them life is safe, but not worth bothering with."

Stephen Fry is an English actor and writer who first rose to prominence as half of the comedic duo Fry and Laurie. Fry has had an illustrious acting career, starring in several award-winning television series and films and winning a Screen Actors Guild Award for his performance in *Gosford Park*. In conjunction with his acting, Fry has published over 20 fiction and nonfiction books to much critical acclaim.

Two Thoughts from
MICHAEL JORDAN

"Some people want it to happen, some wish it would happen, and others make it happen."

"I've failed over and over and over again in my life and that is why I succeed."

Michael Jordan is an American former professional basketball player, widely regarded as one of the greatest players of all time. Jordan's career was marked by numerous accolades, including six NBA championships with the Chicago Bulls and two Olympic gold medals with Team USA. He became a global cultural icon and helped popularize the NBA worldwide in the 1980s and 1990s. Today, Jordan's influence extends beyond the basketball court, and his brand, Air Jordan, is still one of the most popular and influential sneaker lines.

Two Thoughts from

JOHN CLEESE

"He who laughs most, learns best."

"I think the problem with people like this is that they are so stupid that they have no idea how stupid they are."

John Cleese is a British actor, comedian, screenwriter, and producer best known for his work as a member of the surreal comedy group Monty Python. He is the creator and star of the classic British sitcom *Fawlty Towers*. Cleese's unique brand of humor has earned him numerous awards and accolades, and his keen insights on life, intelligence, and comedy continue to resonate with people across generations.

Two Thoughts from
KEN BURNS

"It is the great arrogance of the present to forget the intelligence of the past."

"History doesn't repeat itself, but human nature remains the same."

Ken Burns is an acclaimed American documentary filmmaker known for his comprehensive and expansive explorations of American history. With a distinct visual style that often features the eponymous "Ken Burns effect," his documentaries cover a wide range of subjects, including the Civil War, jazz, and baseball. Burns has received numerous awards and accolades for his work, including the prestigious National Humanities Medal in 1991.

Two Thoughts from

JOHN LENNON

"There's nothing new under the sun. All the roads lead to Rome. And people cannot provide it for you. I can't wake you up. You can wake you up. I can't cure you. You can cure you."

"Life is what happens to you while you're busy making other plans."

John Lennon was an English musician, singer, and songwriter who gained worldwide fame as a member of the Beatles, one of the most successful and influential bands in the history of music. After the Beatles disbanded, Lennon embarked on a successful solo career, becoming known for his social and political activism. Tragically, he was assassinated outside his New York City home in 1980.

Two Thoughts from
DERREN BROWN

"We are terrible at reading each other's thoughts. Yet we consistently behave as if we have been endowed with this entirely handsome ability."

"The sign of the true expert is his modest awareness of how much more there is to know."

Derren Brown is a British mentalist, illusionist, and author. Brown is best known for his television and stage performances that combine magic, suggestion, psychology, and misdirection. He has created several critically acclaimed shows, such as *Trick of the Mind*, *Mind Control*, and *The Heist*. Brown is often praised for his thought-provoking exploration of human behavior and his ability to create seemingly inexplicable phenomena using psychological techniques.

Two Thoughts from

MARILYN MONROE

"Imperfection is beauty, madness is genius and it's better to be absolutely ridiculous than absolutely boring."[10]

"We should all start to live before we get too old. Fear is stupid. So are regrets."

Marilyn Monroe was an iconic American actress, model, and singer who rose to fame in the 1950s and became one of the most recognizable faces in the world. Known for her memorable roles in movies like *Some Like It Hot* and *Gentlemen Prefer Blondes*, Monroe symbolized femininity, sexuality, and glamour in the golden age of Hollywood. Underneath her seemingly perfect facade, Monroe struggled with personal issues throughout her life before tragically passing away at the age of 36.

Two Thoughts from

ALEISTER CROWLEY

"The sin which is unpardonable is knowingly and wilfully to reject truth, to fear knowledge lest that knowledge pander not to thy prejudices."

"There is no law beyond Do what thou wilt."

Aleister Crowley was an English occultist, writer, and founder of the religious movement Thelema. He was an influential figure in the early twentieth century, known for his erratic and controversial behavior and his innovative ideas and practices in Western esotericism, mysticism, and ceremonial magic. Throughout his life, Crowley was also a poet, painter, astrologer, and mountaineer. He was once dubbed the "wickedest man in the world" by the press.

Two Thoughts from

LOUIS ARMSTRONG

"There are some people that if they don't know, you can't tell them."

"A lotta cats copy the Mona Lisa, but people still line up to see the original."

Louis Armstrong, an iconic American jazz musician and singer, was a significant figure in the development of jazz throughout the twentieth century. He achieved tremendous success during his career, both as a trumpet player and as a vocalist. Armstrong's charismatic stage presence, gravelly voice, and innovative improvisational skills left a lasting impact on the world of music. His recordings and collaborations, such as "What a Wonderful World" and "Hello, Dolly!," remain popular to this day.

Two Thoughts from
FREDERICK FRANCK

"It is wise to avoid militants of all plumage, to trust only the fanatically unfanatic."

"The clearsighted eye turns the light back to see its own original nature."

Frederick Franck was a Dutch American painter, sculptor, and writer who authored more than 30 books on art and spirituality. Franck's work can be found in various museums, including the Museum of Modern Art in New York City. His book *The Zen of Seeing* is a classic, with over 300,000 copies in print.

Two Thoughts from

HUGH MACLEOD

"The price of being a sheep is boredom. The price of being a wolf is loneliness. Choose one or the other with great care."

"I work extremely hard doing what I love, mainly to ensure that I don't have to work extremely hard doing what I hate."

Hugh MacLeod is an American artist and author whose artworks can be found in over 5,000 companies around the globe. With Gapingvoid, a marketing blog-turned-company, McLeod has created art for the likes of Intel, Microsoft, and MIT. McLeod has written a number of books on themes of creativity and innovation. One such book, *Ignore Everybody*, which began life as a Gapingvoid blog post, has been downloaded over five million times.

Two Thoughts from
LENNY BRUCE

"The only honest art form is laughter, comedy. You can't fake it. Try to fake three laughs in an hour—ha ha ha ha ha—they'll take you away, man. You can't."

"I was not born in a vacuum. Every thought I have belongs to someone else."

Lenny Bruce was an American stand-up comedian regarded by many as the godfather of countercultural comedy. Known for his edgy comedic style, Bruce was convicted of obscenity in 1964 in what would become a landmark case regarding freedom of speech in the United States. In 2017, *Rolling Stone* ranked Bruce as the third greatest comedian of all time (behind Richard Pryor and George Carlin).

Two Thoughts from
ALEC SOTH

"Nobody really wants to be alone. People need people."

"I always say that photography's closest cousin is poetry because of the way it sparks your imagination and leaves gaps for the viewer to fill in."

Alec Soth is an American photographer and member of the Magnum Photos cooperative. For such published collections as *Sleeping by the Mississippi* and *Niagara*, Soth has received the Santa Fe Prize for Photography and an Honorary Fellowship of the Royal Photographic Society. Today, Soth's photography can be found in the San Francisco Museum of Modern Art; the Museum of Fine Arts, Houston; the Minneapolis Institute of Art; and the Walker Art Center.

Two Thoughts from
BEN HECHT

"Trying to determine what is going on in the world by reading newspapers is like trying to tell the time by watching the second hand of a clock."

"A wise man will always allow a fool to rob him of ideas without yelling 'Thief.'"

Ben Hecht was an American screenwriter, director, producer, playwright, and novelist whose prolific career earned him the nickname "the Shakespeare of Hollywood." He scripted more than 70 films and is considered one of the greatest screenwriters in the history of cinema. Hecht won the first ever Academy Award for Story (now referred to as Best Original Screenplay) for the 1927 movie *Underworld*, and his coauthored book with Charles MacArthur, *The Front Page*, has been adapted for film and radio numerous times.

Two Thoughts from
BILL WATTERSON

"I'm learning skills I will use for the rest of my life by doing homework—procrastinating and negotiation."

"To invent your own life's meaning is not easy, but it's still allowed, and I think you'll be happier for the trouble."

Bill Watterson is an American cartoonist and author best known for his comic strip *Calvin and Hobbes*, which was syndicated from 1985 to 1995. Watterson was awarded the National Cartoonists Society's Reuben Award in both 1986 and 1988; he was the youngest cartoonist ever to win the award and only the sixth person to win twice. In 2014, Watterson became the fourth non-European cartoonist to be awarded the Grand Prix at the Angoulême International Comics Festival.

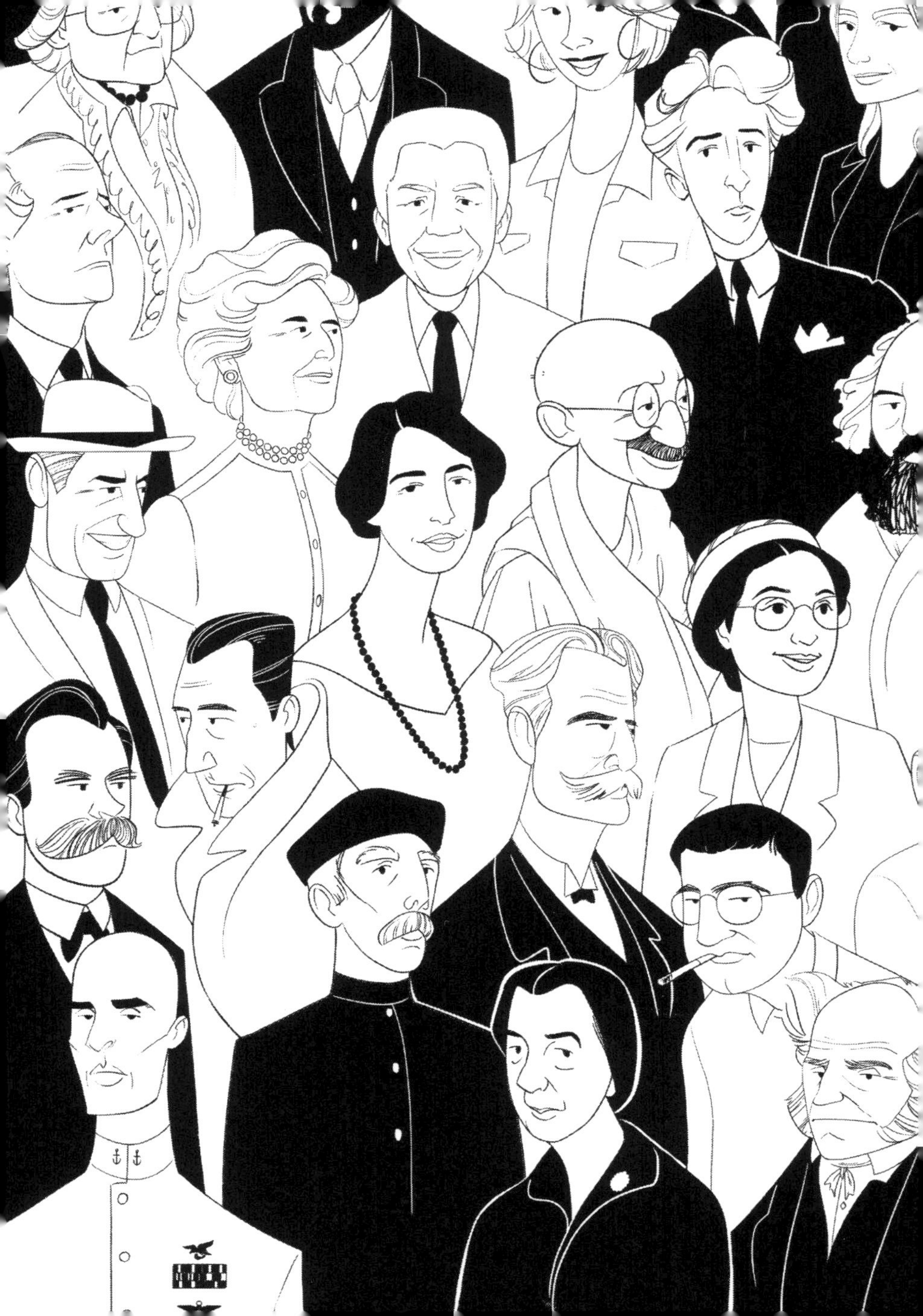

VISIONARIES

philosophers, polymaths,
motivational speakers, political
leaders, spiritual leaders

Two Thoughts from
MARCUS AURELIUS

"If you are distressed by anything external, the pain is not due to the thing itself, but to your estimate of it; and this you have the power to revoke at any moment."

"Don't go on discussing what a good person should be. Just be one."

Marcus Aurelius was a Roman emperor and philosopher who lived during the second century AD. He is also known for his book *Meditations*, which is a personal journal of his reflections on philosophy and morality. His writings are still widely read today and are considered to be a significant influence on Stoic philosophy.

Two Thoughts from

ROSA PARKS

"People always say that I didn't give up my seat because I was tired, but that isn't true. No, the only tired I was, was tired of giving in."

"To bring about change, you must not be afraid to take the first step. We will fail when we fail to try."

Rosa Parks was a pivotal figure in the American civil rights movement, best known for her courageous act in 1955 when she refused to give up her seat to a white passenger on a segregated bus in Montgomery, Alabama. Her arrest sparked the Montgomery Bus Boycott, a landmark event in the fight against racial segregation and a turning point in the broader civil rights movement. Her act of defiance and the subsequent boycott lasted over a year and resulted in the US Supreme Court ruling that segregation on public buses was unconstitutional. Rosa Parks's legacy as the "mother of the civil rights movement" reflects her lifelong commitment to social justice and equality.

Two Thoughts from

FRIEDRICH NIETZSCHE

"Whoever fights monsters should see to it that in the process he does not become a monster. And if you gaze long enough into an abyss, the abyss will gaze back into you."

"Convictions are more dangerous foes of truth than lies."

Friedrich Nietzsche was a German philosopher, cultural critic, poet, and philologist. He is best known for his critiques of traditional morality and religion, and his ideas have had a profound influence on modern philosophy and intellectual history.

Two Thoughts from

BENJAMIN FRANKLIN

"Many people die at 25 and aren't buried until they are 75."[11]

"Never confuse motion with action."

Benjamin Franklin was one of the Founding Fathers of the United States, a polymath, and a statesman. He is known for his numerous inventions, including the lightning rod, bifocal glasses, and the Franklin stove. He was also an author, printer, and diplomat. His wit and wisdom have made him one of the most quoted figures in American history.

Two Thoughts from
LEONARDO DA VINCI

"The greatest deception men suffer is from their own opinions."

"One can have no smaller or greater mastery than mastery of oneself."

Leonardo da Vinci was an Italian polymath who lived during the Renaissance period. He was a painter, sculptor, architect, musician, scientist, mathematician, engineer, inventor, anatomist, geologist, cartographer, botanist, and writer. He is widely considered one of the most diversely talented individuals to have ever lived, and his artistic and scientific contributions have had a lasting impact on human history.

Two Thoughts from

ARTHUR SCHOPENHAUER

"All truth passes through three stages. First, it is ridiculed. Second, it is violently opposed. Third, it is accepted as being self-evident."

"Talent hits a target no one else can hit; genius hits a target no one else can see."

Arthur Schopenhauer was a German philosopher who is best known for his pessimistic worldview and philosophical essays. He was heavily influenced by Eastern philosophy and is often associated with the philosophical movement of existentialism. Schopenhauer's work explores the nature of human suffering and the human condition.

Two Thoughts from
EPICTETUS

"There is only one way to happiness and that is to cease worrying about things which are beyond the power of our will."

"It is impossible for a man to learn what he thinks he already knows."

Epictetus was a Greek Stoic philosopher who lived in the first century AD. His philosophy emphasizes personal ethics and the importance of living a virtuous life. Epictetus believed that individuals should focus on the things that are within their control, and that true happiness comes from finding life's purpose, accepting one's fate, and behaving morally regardless of the personal cost.

Two Thoughts from

DON MIGUEL RUIZ

"Whatever happens around you, don't take it personally...Nothing other people do is because of you. It is because of themselves."

"Be impeccable with your word. Don't take anything personally. Don't make assumptions. Always do your best."

Don Miguel Ruiz is a Mexican author and Toltec spiritualist. His work aligns with some principles of the New Thought movement, which focuses on ancient teachings as a means to achieve spiritual enlightenment. In 1997, Ruiz marked his authorial debut with the publication of *The Four Agreements*, which would remain a *New York Times* bestseller for over a decade.

Two Thoughts from

ALBERT CAMUS

"The need to be right is the sign of a vulgar mind."

"Man is the only creature that refuses to be what he is."

Albert Camus was a French writer and philosopher, often regarded as one of the leading figures in twentieth-century absurdist and existentialist thought. In equal parts an author, playwright, and essayist, Camus is perhaps best known for a philosophical work entitled *The Myth of Sisyphus*. In 1957, Camus was awarded the Nobel Prize for Literature: the second-youngest recipient in the category's history.

Two Thoughts from

ALEXANDER VON HUMBOLDT

"I am more and more convinced that our happiness or unhappiness depends more on the way we meet the events of life than on the nature of those events themselves."

"How a person masters his fate is more important than what his fate is."

Alexander von Humboldt was a German polymath, geographer, naturalist, explorer, and philosopher. Humboldt's five-volume *Cosmos*, which was published between 1845 and 1862, kickstarted the popularization of science as a vocation. In terms of legacy, his botanical work laid the foundations for the field of biogeography, while his advocacy for quantitative analysis paved the way for modern geomagnetic and meteorological monitoring.

Two Thoughts from
THOMAS PAINE

"A hereditary monarch is as absurd a position as a hereditary doctor or mathematician."

"What we obtain too cheaply, we esteem too lightly; it's dearness only that gives everything its value."

Thomas Paine was an English American writer and political reformer whose pamphlet "Common Sense" would become foundational during the early days of the American Revolution. Following a stint in prison, Paine published his best-selling work, *The Age of Reason*, in three parts in 1794, 1795, and 1807, which appealed for the separation of church and state. Paine's work inspired and guided many free thinkers.

Two Thoughts from

MAHATMA GANDHI

"Be the change that you wish to see in the world."

"The simplest acts of kindness are by far more powerful than a thousand heads bowing in prayer."

Mohandas Karamchand Gandhi was an Indian lawyer and a national and spiritual leader who employed nonviolent resistance in the fight for India's independence from British rule. His philosophy of nonviolence, known as Satyagraha, inspired civil rights and freedom movements across the world. In 1915, poet and Nobel laureate Rabindranath Tagore bestowed on Gandhi the title "Mahatma," meaning "great-souled."

Two Thoughts from
DENIS DIDEROT

"We swallow greedily any lie that flatters us, but we sip only little by little at a truth we find bitter."

"All things must be examined, debated, investigated without exception and without regard for anyone's feelings."

Denis Diderot was a French philosopher and writer best known as the creator of the *Encyclopédie*, a general encyclopedia published between 1751 and 1772. Historians have proffered the publication of the radically empirical *Encyclopédie* as a precursor to the French Revolution. Alongside Voltaire, Diderot has come to be regarded as a paradigmatic example of the French Enlightenment philosopher.

Two Thoughts from

ELEANOR ROOSEVELT

"No one can make you feel inferior without your consent."

"A good leader inspires people to have confidence in the leader. A great leader inspires people to have confidence in themselves."

Eleanor Roosevelt was an American political figure, diplomat, and activist who served as the First Lady of the United States from 1933 to 1945. Roosevelt was a strong advocate for civil rights, women's rights, and human rights, and was instrumental in shaping global policy in these areas. She was also a prolific writer, penning several books and columns on politics and social issues. The last of her "My Day" columns appeared just weeks before her death in 1962.

Two Thoughts from

FRANCIS BACON

"Man prefers to believe what he prefers to be true."

"If we are to achieve things never before accomplished we must employ methods never before attempted."

Francis Bacon was an English statesman and philosopher, often regarded as the father of empiricism. In *The New Organon* as well as in his essays, Bacon laid the foundation for natural philosophy and the scientific method, becoming a pivotal figure in the Scientific Revolution. Writing aside, Bacon served as the lord chancellor of England from 1618 to 1621.

Two Thoughts from

WILLIAM ARTHUR WARD

"Feeling gratitude and not expressing it is like wrapping a present and not giving it."

"Today is a most unusual day, because we have never lived it before; we will never live it again; it is the only day we have."

William Arthur Ward was an American author, educator, and motivational speaker known for his vast collection of inspiring quotes and sayings. He has been recognized for his work in the fields of personal growth, development, and success. Ward's quotes often touch on themes such as gratitude, individual potential, and seizing the moment with positivity.

Two Thoughts from

NELSON MANDELA

"May your choices reflect your hopes, not your fears."

"Resentment is like drinking poison and then hoping it will kill your enemies."

Nelson Mandela was a South African politician and civil rights activist whose opposition to apartheid would lead to 27 years in prison. Upon release, Mandela ultimately brought an end to racial segregation in South Africa, serving as the country's first president from 1994 to 1999. Alongside F. W. de Clerk, Mandela was awarded the Nobel Peace Prize in 1993.

Two Thoughts from
CARL VON CLAUSEWITZ

"Many intelligence reports in war are contradictory; even more are false, and most are uncertain."

"The enemy of a good plan is the dream of a perfect plan."

Carl von Clausewitz was a Prussian military general and theorist best known for his book *On War*, which influenced military strategy, politics, and international relations for more than a century. Clausewitz's experiences while serving during the Napoleonic Wars inspired him to create theories on the nature of warfare and formulate innovative strategic principles. Today, his work is still studied by military professionals and political leaders worldwide.

Two Thoughts from

ZHUANG ZHOU (ZHUANGZI)

"When the heart is right, 'for' and 'against' are forgotten."

"Great wisdom is generous; petty wisdom is contentious."

Zhuang Zhou, also known as Zhuangzi, was an ancient Chinese philosopher who lived during the Warring States period around the fourth century BCE. He is considered one of the foundational figures of Taoism and is credited with authoring the influential text known as the *Zhuangzi*, which explores topics including the nature of reality, the limitations of human knowledge, and the importance of spontaneous, natural action. His teachings emphasize the importance of living in harmony with the Tao (the natural way of the cosmos) and often use parables and anecdotes to illustrate his points.

Two Thoughts from
MARY MIDGLEY

"Our dominant technology shapes our symbolism and thereby our metaphysics, our view about what is real."

"None of us can study anything properly unless we do it with our whole being."

Mary Midgley was a British philosopher known for her insightful works on the relationship between science, ethics, and human nature. She authored numerous books like *Beast and Man*, *Animals and Why They Matter*, and *Evolution as a Religion*, addressing topics like animal rights, the environment, and the philosophy of science. Midgley was recognized for her ability to tackle complex ideas with clarity and wit, and her work has been influential in both academic and public spheres.

Two Thoughts from
JAMES ALLEN

"The more tranquil a man becomes, the greater is his success, his influence, his power for good. Calmness of mind is one of the beautiful jewels of wisdom."

"Circumstances do not make the man, they reveal him."

James Allen was a British writer and philosopher whose explorations of inspiration and motivation would lay the foundations for self-help as a literary genre. First published in 1903, *As a Man Thinketh* skyrocketed Allen to worldwide fame as a prophet of inspirational thinking, and remains a perennial classic of the self-help genre.

Two Thoughts from

MICHAEL A. SINGER

"In order to be who you are, you must be willing to let go of who you think you are."

"Only you can take inner freedom away from yourself, or give it to yourself. Nobody else can."

Michael A. Singer is an American author and spiritual teacher best known for his books *The Untethered Soul* and *The Surrender Experiment*. His works focus on personal growth, spiritual awakening, and mindfulness. In addition to his writing, Singer has made significant contributions to the field of medical software, and he cofounded Medical Manager, now called Greenway Health.

Two Thoughts from

JIM HIGHTOWER

"The opposite for courage is not cowardice, it is conformity. Even a dead fish can go with the flow."

"America was not built by conformists, but by mutineers."

Jim Hightower is an American populist, author, radio commentator, and political activist who is known for his humorous wit and blunt take on politics. A former elected Texas agricultural commissioner, Hightower has dedicated his life to challenging the power of moneyed interests and fighting for everyday people. Throughout his career, he has utilized his distinct voice in various forms, including books, newsletters, and his nationally syndicated radio show, *Hightower Radio*.

Two Thoughts from
ALEXANDER THE GREAT

"A tomb now suffices him for whom the whole world was not sufficient."

"I am not afraid of an army of lions led by a sheep, I am afraid of an army of sheep led by a lion."

Alexander the Great was a king of Macedonia who, through his military prowess and strategic genius, created one of the largest empires in the ancient world by the age of 30. Known for his relentless ambition and drive, he conquered vast territories stretching from Greece to Egypt and as far east as modern-day Pakistan. Alexander is celebrated for spreading Greek culture, founding numerous cities, and blending Eastern and Western ideals through his conquests.

Two Thoughts from
THOMAS JEFFERSON

"I never considered a difference of opinion in politics, in religion, in philosophy, as cause for withdrawing from a friend."

"How much pain have cost us the evils which have never happened."

Thomas Jefferson was an American philosopher and statesman who served as the third president of the United States. Of all the Founding Fathers, Jefferson has come to be regarded as America's most distinguished "apostle of liberty." Among his many accomplishments, Jefferson drafted the Declaration of Independence, founded the University of Virginia, and negotiated the Louisiana Purchase. The Jefferson Memorial was founded in Washington, D.C., on April 13, 1943, the 200th anniversary of his birth.

Two Thoughts from
ALBERT SCHWEITZER

"Do something wonderful, people may imitate it."

"There are only three ways to teach a child. The first is by example, the second is by example, the third is by example."

Albert Schweitzer was a French German philosopher, physician, and musician who dedicated his life to promoting humanitarian causes. He influenced numerous fields, such as theology, organ music, and animal rights. He was awarded the Nobel Peace Prize in 1952 for the "Reverence for Life" concept in his philosophy. Schweitzer established and managed a medical mission in Africa and inspired countless individuals through his compassionate approach to living.

Two Thoughts from
HERACLITUS

"The content of your character is your choice. Day by day, what you choose, what you think and what you do is who you become."

"Those who love wisdom must investigate many things."

Heraclitus was a pre-Socratic Greek philosopher. He was known for his thoughts on the unity of opposites and his doctrine of change being central to the universe. He was active around 500 BCE and is known as the "Weeping Philosopher" due to the often-somber nature of his ideas. Heraclitus believed that fire was the ultimate and original element and the basis of all other elements in the universe.

Two Thoughts from
GOLDA MEIR

"One cannot and must not try to erase the past merely because it does not fit the present."

"It is always much easier, I have discovered, to make people cry or gasp than to make them think."

Golda Meir was an Israeli stateswoman, political leader, and the fourth prime minister of Israel. Born in Kiev in 1898 and raised in Milwaukee, Wisconsin, Meir emigrated to Palestine in 1921, where she became actively involved in the Zionist movement. As prime minister from 1969 to 1974, she navigated tumultuous times, including the 1972 Munich Olympics massacre and the Yom Kippur War in 1973. Meir was one of the first women to lead a modern state and was often referred to affectionately as the "Iron Lady" of Israeli politics. She resigned in 1974 and passed away in 1978, leaving a lasting legacy in Israeli history.

Two Thoughts from
JAMES MADISON

"The truth is that all men having power ought to be mistrusted."

"The advancement and diffusion of knowledge is the only guardian of true liberty."

James Madison was an American statesman, political theorist, and the fourth president of the United States. Known as the "father of the Constitution," Madison played a pivotal role in drafting and promoting the United States Constitution and the Bill of Rights. Alongside his close friends Thomas Jefferson and Alexander Hamilton, Madison was a key figure in the establishment of a modern and stable government in the United States, and his contributions to political theory and practice continue to shape the nation.

Two Thoughts from

EKNATH EASWARAN

"When someone at peace and free from hurry enters a room, that person has a calming effect on everyone present."

"Patience can't be acquired overnight. It is just like building up a muscle. Every day you need to work on it."

Eknath Easwaran was an Indian author and spiritual teacher who published 40 books on meditation and religion over the course of his life. During his time teaching courses on mediation at the University of California, Berkeley, Easwaran developed the practice of Passage Meditation, which revolves around the silent repetition of passages from the world's major religious texts.

Two Thoughts from

DAVID GOGGINS

"The only thing more contagious than a good attitude is a bad one."

"Denial is the ultimate comfort zone."

David Goggins is a retired **Navy SEAL**, ultramarathon runner, and motivational speaker widely recognized for his incredible mental resilience and determination. Goggins has completed several extreme endurance challenges including the Badwater Ultramarathon, and he holds the world record for most pull-ups in 24 hours. He is also the author of the best-selling book *Can't Hurt Me*, which chronicles his life story and shares his insights on overcoming obstacles and achieving personal goals.

Two Thoughts from

FREDERICK THE GREAT

"The greatest and noblest pleasure which men can have in this world is to discover new truths; and the next is to shake off old prejudices."

"He who cannot stand misfortune does not deserve good fortune."

Frederick the Great, also known as Frederick II, was the king of Prussia from 1740 to 1786. Known for his military successes, he was a patron of the arts and advanced the cause of Enlightenment, earning the title "Enlightened Despot." Frederick the Great was a skilled musician, philosopher, and writer, and he introduced significant reforms in his kingdom, such as religious tolerance, legal and bureaucratic improvements, and the promotion of education.

Two Thoughts from
JIM ROHN

"Formal education will make you a living; self-education will make you a fortune."

"Your personal philosophy is the greatest determining factor in how your life works out."

Jim Rohn was an influential American entrepreneur, author, and motivational speaker. Known for his exceptional communication skills, he mentored and inspired numerous individuals throughout his career, including fellow author and motivational speaker Tony Robbins. Rohn was recognized for his enlightening ideas on personal development, self-education, and having a life-changing personal philosophy.

Two Thoughts from
SØREN KIERKEGAARD

"Life can only be understood backwards, but it must be lived forwards."

"What labels me, negates me."

Søren Kierkegaard was a Danish philosopher. He is widely regarded as the father of existentialism. Unlike many of his contemporaries, Kierkegaard worked toward a philosophy of the individual, favoring concrete reality over abstract thought. His works, such as *Fear and Trembling* and *Either/Or*, remain classics to this day.

Two Thoughts from
SLAVOJ ŽIŽEK

"We feel free because we lack the very language to articulate our unfreedom."

"The threat today is not passivity, but pseudo-activity, the urge to 'be active,' to 'participate,' to mask the nothingness of what goes on."

Slavoj Žižek is a Slovenian philosopher, psychoanalyst, and cultural critic, widely recognized for his insightful and provocative social analysis. He has been the international director of the Birkbeck Institute of Humanities and has written extensively on topics such as ideology, capitalism, and the environment. Žižek's unique blend of philosophy, psychoanalysis, and popular culture has earned him a substantial following and the label "the Elvis of cultural theory."

Two Thoughts from

MARSHALL MCLUHAN

"We become what we behold. We shape our tools, and thereafter our tools shape us."[12]

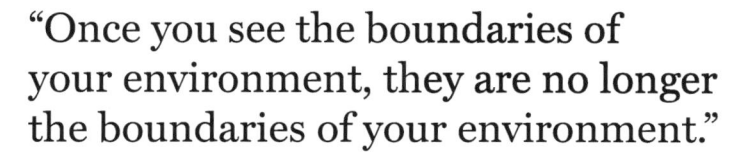

"Once you see the boundaries of your environment, they are no longer the boundaries of your environment."

Marshall McLuhan was a Canadian philosopher and professor widely recognized for his pioneering work in media theory and communications studies. He is best known for coining the phrase "the medium is the message," which emphasized the importance of examining not only the content but also the form of communication to understand its influence on society. McLuhan's ideas influenced various fields, including advertising, journalism, and education, and his theories remain relevant in the age of digital media and rapid technological advancement.

Two Thoughts from
BRENÉ BROWN

"If you trade your authenticity for safety, you may experience the following: anxiety, depression, eating disorders, addiction, rage, blame, resentment, and inexplicable grief."

"Curiosity is a shit-starter."

Brené Brown is an American professor, author, and public speaker renowned for her research on vulnerability, courage, empathy, and shame. She is the author of many #1 *New York Times* bestsellers, and her 2010 TEDxHouston talk, "The Power of Vulnerability," has become one of the most-watched talks on the TED.com platform, with over 50 million views. In 2019, Brown's Netflix special *Brené Brown: The Call to Courage* debuted, further spreading her message about embracing vulnerability and authenticity in our lives.

Two Thoughts from
SAMUEL ADAMS

"We cannot make events. Our business is wisely to improve them."

"How strangely will the Tools of a Tyrant pervert the plain Meaning of Words!"

Samuel Adams was a statesman and Founding Father of the United States. Beginning his political career in Massachusetts, Adams became a leader of the American Revolution and was a signatory of the Declaration of Independence in 1776. Adams later served as governor of Massachusetts from 1794 to 1797.

Two Thoughts from
FRIEDRICH SCHELLING

"This is not the time to reawaken old oppositions, but rather to seek what lies above and beyond all opposition."

"All rules for study are summed up in this one: learn only in order to create."

Friedrich Schelling was a German philosopher regarded as a significant figure of German idealism in post-Kantian thought. Though he was a college roommate of Hegel, Schelling's critique of Hegelian idealism influenced the likes of Kierkegaard, Marx, Nietzsche, and Heidegger. His *Naturphilosophie* has been criticized by the scientific community for the lack of an empirical orientation, but Schelling himself remains a key figure within philosophy.

Two Thoughts from
KARL POPPER

"True ignorance is not the absence of knowledge, but the refusal to acquire it."

"In so far as a scientific statement speaks about reality, it must be falsifiable: and in so far as it is not falsifiable, it does not speak about reality."

Karl Popper was an Austrian-born British philosopher and professor known for his significant contributions to the philosophy of science and political philosophy. He is best remembered for introducing the concept of falsifiability as a scientific criterion, as well as for advocating a critical rationalist methodology. Popper's work, such as *The Logic of Scientific Discovery* and *The Open Society and Its Enemies*, profoundly impacted the scientific and political thinking of the twentieth century.

Two Thoughts from

JOHANN WOLFGANG VON GOETHE

"You can easily judge the character of a man by how he treats those who can do nothing for him."[13]

"Knowing is not enough, we must apply. Willing is not enough, we must do."

Johann Wolfgang von Goethe was a German writer, poet, and philosopher who had an immense influence on Western literature and thought. Among his numerous achievements, Goethe's most renowned work is the tragic play *Faust*, considered a cornerstone of world literature. He was also a respected scientist who conducted research in various fields, including plant morphology and color theory. Goethe's works touched on multiple aspects of human nature, often emphasizing the importance of personal development, ethics, and action.

Two Thoughts from

GUY DEBORD

"In our society now, we prefer to see ourselves living than living."

"Quotations are useful in periods of ignorance or obscurantist beliefs."

Guy Debord was a French Marxist theorist, philosopher, and filmmaker who was a founding member of the Situationist International. This avant-garde movement influenced the May 1968 protests in France, where more than 10 million people participated in a general strike against capitalism, imperialism, and the French government. Debord's work focused on spectacle and power dynamics in social and political life and the role of art in society. His book *The Society of the Spectacle* has become a seminal work in critical theory.

Two Thoughts from
JOSÉ ORTEGA Y GASSET

"Life is a series of collisions with the future; it is not the sum of what we have been, but what we yearn to be."

"Our firmest convictions are apt to be the most suspect; they mark our limitations and our bounds."

José Ortega y Gasset was a renowned Spanish philosopher and essayist. He is widely regarded as one of the most prominent intellectuals of the twentieth century. Known for expounding upon "perspectivism" as well as the concept of "razón vital" (vital reason), his work explored the human experience and the role individuals play in shaping reality. Continuously in print since 1932, his book *The Revolt of the Masses* explores the rise of the "mass-man" who, "in face of any problem, is satisfied with thinking the first thing he finds in his head."

Two Thoughts from
GILBERT RYLE

"The vain man does not think he is vain."

"Chronicles are not explanatory of what they record."

Gilbert Ryle was a British philosopher who served as president of the Aristotelian Society from 1945 to 1946. Ryle is perhaps best known for his critique of Cartesian dualism, which would give rise to the phrase "ghost in the machine." His most famous book, *The Concept of Mind*, remains a cornerstone of the philosophical canon.

Two Thoughts from
MICHEL DE MONTAIGNE

"How many things served us yesterday for articles of faith, which today are fables for us?"

"I speak the truth, not so much as I would, but as much as I dare; and I dare a little more as I grow older."

Michel de Montaigne was a French philosopher and essayist whose writings became a cornerstone of the French Renaissance. Known for his unusually anecdotal and autobiographical style, Montaigne is celebrated for the quality of his essays and for establishing the essay as a literary genre. His magnum opus, *Essais*, remains one of the most influential books ever written.

Two Thoughts from

CRISS JAMI

"At first, they'll only dislike what you say, but the more correct you start sounding the more they'll dislike you."

"There's nothing more contagious than the laughter of young children; it doesn't even have to matter what they're laughing about."

Criss Jami is an American writer and polymath who has published several books of philosophy and poetry, most notably *Killosophy*. Having studied philosophy at George Mason University, Jami has since turned his attention to music and fashion, channeling his creativity through his heavy metal project, Crymson Gryphon, and his clothing line, Killosopher Apparel.

Two Thoughts from
BARBARA BUSH

"Bias has to be taught. If you hear your parents downgrading women or people of different backgrounds, why, you are going to do that."

"The Titanic was built by professionals. The Ark was built by volunteers."

Barbara Bush was a former First Lady of the United States and founder of the Barbara Bush Foundation for Family Literacy. The wife of George H. W. Bush, she was also the mother of George W. Bush, who served as the 43rd president of the United States. In terms of legacy, Bush has been celebrated for her promotion of literacy and her support for people living with AIDS.

Two Thoughts from

THOMAS FREY

"Every avalanche begins with the movement of a single snowflake, and my hope is to move a snowflake."

"Thinking about the future will cause it to change."

Thomas Frey is an American futurist and public speaker, currently serving as the cofounder and executive director of the Da Vinci Institute. Before launching the Da Vinci Institute, Frey spent 15 years as an engineer and designer at IBM, where he received over 270 awards—more than any other IBM engineer. As part of the celebrity speaking circuit, Frey has given keynote speeches at the likes of NASA, Disney, Visa, and TED.

Two Thoughts from
VÁCLAV HAVEL

"Keep the company of those who seek the truth—run from those who have found it."

"Vision is not enough, it must be combined with venture. It is not enough to stare up the steps, we must step up the stairs."

Václav Havel was a Czech statesman and author who served as the first democratically elected president of Czechoslovakia and the Czech Republic after the fall of communism. Havel received numerous accolades for his political activism, including the Presidential Medal of Freedom and the Gandhi Peace Prize. Outside of politics, Havel was an accomplished playwright and poet, becoming an Honorary Fellow of the Royal Society of Literature in 1993.

Two Thoughts from

JEAN COCTEAU

"We must believe in luck. For how else can we explain the success of those we don't like?"

"Statues to great men are made of the stones thrown at them in their lifetime."

Jean Cocteau was a French writer and artist. He is regarded as a central figure within the surrealist, avant-garde, and Dadaist movements. Some of Cocteau's most celebrated works include the poem "L'Ange Heurtebise," the play *Orphée*, and the novel *Les Enfants Terribles*. During World War I, Cocteau served as an ambulance driver on the Belgian front.

Two Thoughts from
BALTASAR GRACIÁN

"There's no greater absurdity than taking everything seriously."

"Never compete with someone who has nothing to lose."

Baltasar Gracián was a Spanish Jesuit and philosopher. He is regarded as a founding father of conceptism, or *conceptismo*, a brash and aphoristic style of writing. In 1992, almost four centuries after its original release, a new translation of Gracián's *The Art of Worldly Wisdom* became a national bestseller in the United States, selling almost 200,000 copies.

Two Thoughts from
BRIAN TRACY

"The more credit you give away, the more will come back to you. The more you help others, the more they will want to help you."

"Never say anything about yourself you don't want to come true."

Brian Tracy is an American author and motivational speaker. He is currently the chairman and CEO of Brian Tracy International. The author of over 50 books, such as *Earn What You're Really Worth* and *Eat That Frog!*, Tracy has had his work translated into dozens of languages. As a motivational speaker, Tracy has given more than 5,000 talks and seminars in upwards of 70 countries around the world.

Two Thoughts from

MIKHAIL BAKUNIN

"The urge for destruction is also a creative urge!"

"If you took the most ardent revolutionary, vested him in absolute power, within a year he would be worse than the Tsar himself."

Mikhail Bakunin was a Russian revolutionary and writer who is remembered as a major figure in the history of anarchism. After participating in the 1848 Prague and 1849 Dresden uprisings, Bakunin was imprisoned, tried, and exiled to Siberia. Published posthumously, his major work, *God and the State*, has been widely translated and remains in print to this day.

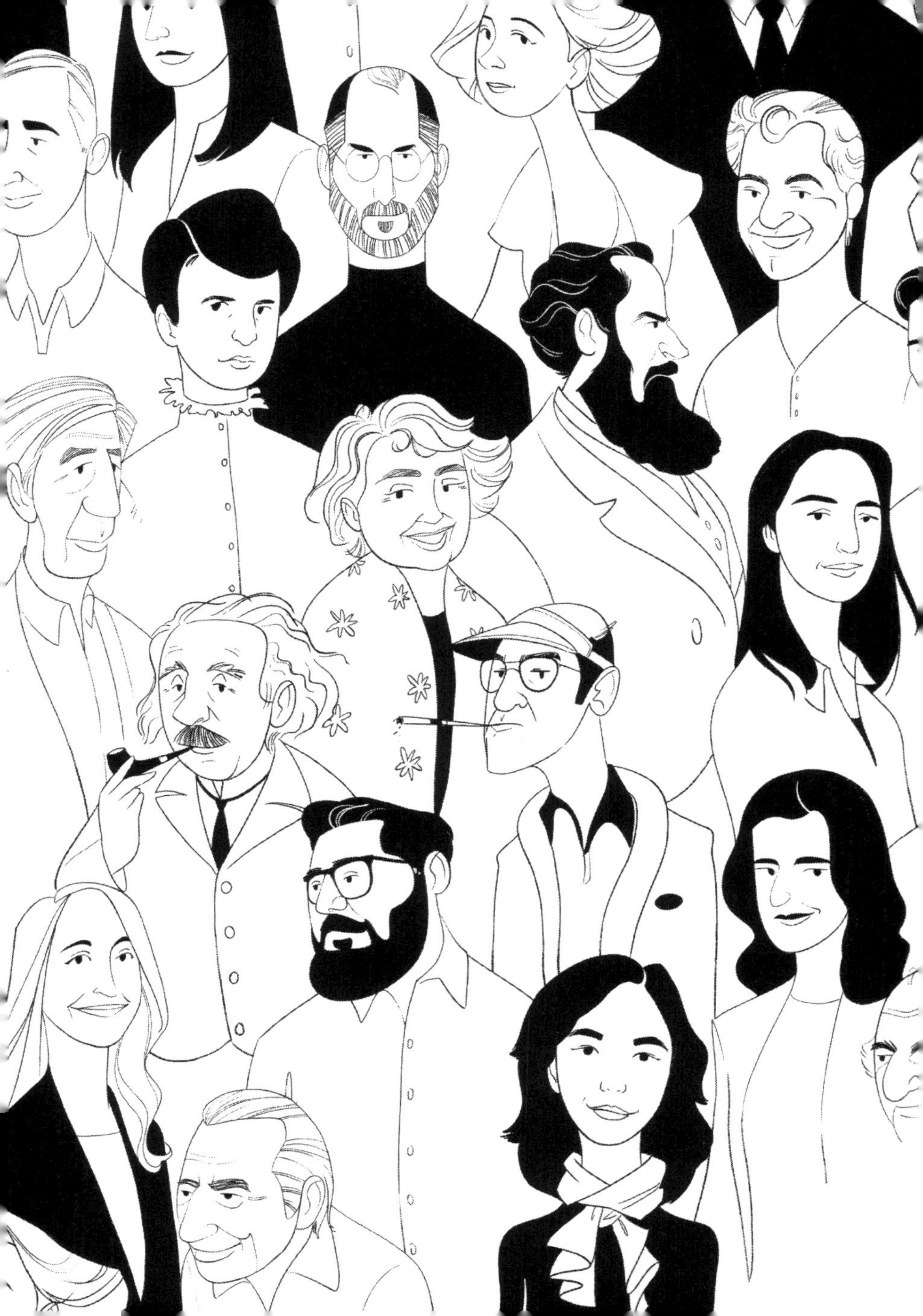

INNOVATORS

scientists, entrepreneurs,
engineers, inventors,
journalists

Two Thoughts from
ALBERT EINSTEIN

"Unthinking respect for authority is the greatest enemy of truth."

"I must be willing to give up what I am in order to become what I will be."

Albert Einstein was a German-born theoretical physicist who is widely considered to be one of the most influential scientists of the twentieth century. He is known for developing the theory of general relativity and his famous equation $E = mc^2$, which describes the relationship between mass and energy. Einstein was also an outspoken pacifist and civil rights advocate.

Two Thoughts from
CARLO ROVELLI

"Albert Einstein spent a year loafing aimlessly. You don't get anywhere by not wasting time—something, unfortunately, that the parents of teenagers tend frequently to forget."

"You don't get to new places by following established tracks."

Carlo Rovelli is an Italian author and theoretical physicist. His work is largely focused on quantum gravity, and he is a founder of loop quantum gravity theory. His third book, *Seven Brief Lessons on Physics*, has been translated into 41 languages and has sold over a million copies worldwide. In 2019, *Foreign Policy* magazine named Rovelli as one of the 100 most influential thinkers in the world.

Two Thoughts from
TARA SWART

"Reassessing our own 'failures' and rebranding them as 'not yets' is a good way to start rewriting our own story: the internal narrative of our past struggles."

"Note to self: we do not have to be slaves to our chronological age!"

Tara Swart is a British neuroscientist and senior lecturer at MIT Sloan whose work focuses on the role of neuroplasticity in **self-care** and transformation. Her latest book, *The Source*, is an international bestseller and has translations in 38 global territories. Outside of neuroscience, Swart is a trustee at the Lady Garden Foundation, a charity focused on gynecological cancer.

Two Thoughts from
J. P. MORGAN

"There's nothing in this world which will so violently distort a man's judgment more than the sight of his neighbor getting rich."

"When you expect things to happen—strangely enough—they do happen."

J. P. Morgan was an American financier and investment banker who rose to prominence on Wall Street in the decades leading up to the turn of the twentieth century (known as the Gilded Age). Morgan had a profound effect on American history: he was the mastermind behind much of the American railway, the consolidator of United States Steel and General Electric, and the stock-market savior of the "Panic of 1907."

Two Thoughts from
HERBERT A. SIMON

"A wealth of information creates a poverty of attention."

"You do not change people's minds by defeating them with logic."

Herbert A. Simon was an American scientist and theorist whose work encompassed computer science, economics, and cognitive psychology. A pioneer in the field of AI, Simon is best remembered for coining the concepts of "bounded rationality" and "satisficing," which would ultimately lead Simon to both a Nobel Prize and a Turing Award.

Two Thoughts from

NIKOLA TESLA

"All that was great in the past was ridiculed, condemned, combated, suppressed—only to emerge all the more powerfully, all the more triumphantly from the struggle."

"We are all one. Only egos, beliefs, and fears separate us."

Nikola Tesla was a Serbian American inventor, electrical engineer, and futurist. Tesla is best known for his contributions to the design of the modern alternating current (AC) electricity supply system. Tesla was a brilliant innovator who had a deep understanding of science and technology, and his ideas continue to influence modern physics and engineering.

Two Thoughts from

MARIE CURIE

"Nothing in life is to be feared, it is only to be understood. Now is the time to understand more, so that we may fear less."

"Be less curious about people and more curious about ideas."

Marie Curie was a Polish French physicist and chemist who is best known for her pioneering work in the field of radioactivity. She was the first woman to be awarded a Nobel Prize and the first person to win two Nobel Prizes in different fields. Curie's work created a new field of study, atomic physics, and laid the foundation for many scientific advancements. Curie herself coined the term "radioactivity."

Two Thoughts from

CHRISTOPHER HITCHENS

"That which can be asserted without evidence, can be dismissed without evidence."

"The essence of the independent mind lies not in what it thinks, but in how it thinks."

Christopher Hitchens was a British American journalist and author whose scathing critiques of religion and politics cemented his status as one of the foremost provocateurs of the twentieth century. A prolific author, Hitchens wrote or edited over 30 books, the controversial titles of which included *God Is Not Great: How Religion Poisons Everything* and *The Missionary Position: Mother Teresa in Theory and Practice*. Throughout his life, Hitchens remained a staunch defender of free expression and scientific discovery.

Two Thoughts from
FRANCIS CRICK

"In spite of the steady accumulation of detailed knowledge, how the human brain works is still profoundly mysterious."

"Avoid the temptation to work so hard that there is no time left for serious thinking."

Francis Crick was a British molecular biologist, biophysicist, and neuroscientist. He is best known for the paper he co-authored with James Watson that proposed the double helix structure of DNA. In 1962, Crick and Watson, along with Maurice Wilkins, were awarded the Nobel Prize in Physiology or Medicine. For the remainder of his career, Crick held the post of J.W. Kieckhefer Distinguished Research Professor at the Salk Institute for Biological Studies in La Jolla, California.

Two Thoughts from

HUNTER S. THOMPSON

"A man who procrastinates in his choosing will inevitably have his choice made for him by circumstance."

"Life has become immeasurably better since I have been forced to stop taking it seriously."

Hunter S. Thompson was an American journalist and author known for his unconventional writing style and books including *Hell's Angels* and *Fear and Loathing in Las Vegas*. He was a prominent figure in the counterculture of the 1960s and 1970s and was known for his political and social commentary.

Two Thoughts from
PETER THIEL

"Indefinite fears about the far future shouldn't stop us from making definite plans today."

"If you think something hard is impossible, you'll never even start trying to achieve it."

Peter Thiel is a German American entrepreneur and venture capitalist best known as the cofounder of PayPal, Palantir Technologies, and Founders Fund. His investment portfolio includes the first outside investment in Facebook. Thiel has since become known for his philanthropic work, most notably through Breakout Labs, which funds nonprofit research into AI and life extension, and the Thiel Fellowship, which provides grants to aspiring entrepreneurs.

Two Thoughts from
STEPHEN HAWKING

"One of the basic rules of the universe is that nothing is perfect. Perfection simply doesn't exist. Without imperfection, neither you nor I would exist."

"Intelligence is the ability to adapt to change."

Stephen Hawking was an English theoretical physicist and author whose work on the origins of the universe—specifically, the Big Bang and exploding black holes—revolutionized the field. His popular science book on the subject, *A Brief History of Time*, has sold more than 25 million copies to date, and appeared on the *Sunday Times* bestseller list for a record-breaking 237 weeks. From 1979 to 2009, Hawking served as the Lucasian Professor of Mathematics at the University of Cambridge, often regarded as the most prestigious academic position in the world.

Two Thoughts from
JOHN VON NEUMANN

"There's no sense in being precise when you don't even know what you're talking about."

"If people do not believe that mathematics is simple, it is only because they do not realize how complicated life is."

John von Neumann was a Hungarian American mathematician, physicist, and computer scientist. He made fundamental contributions to a wide range of fields, including game theory, quantum mechanics, and computer architecture. Von Neumann is considered one of the greatest mathematicians of the twentieth century and, along with Alan Turing and Claude Shannon, was a key figure in the development of the modern computer.

Two Thoughts from
HELEN CZERSKI

"Humans, we're not aware of the ultraviolet light in the first place, so we don't lose anything when it gets turned into something we can use."

"A scientific hypothesis must make specific testable predictions."

Helen Czerski is a British physicist and oceanographer who graduated with a PhD in experimental explosives physics from the University of Cambridge. A regular contributor to the BBC, Czerski has presented the likes of *Orbit: Earth's Extraordinary Journey* and the *Royal Institution Christmas Lectures*. In 2018, Czerski was awarded the William Thomson, Lord Kelvin Medal and Prize from the Institute of Physics.

Two Thoughts from
ERWIN SCHRÖDINGER

"The task is not so much to see what no one has yet seen, but to think what nobody has yet thought, about that which everybody sees."[14]

"If a man never contradicts himself, the reason must be that he virtually never says anything at all."

Erwin Schrödinger was an Austrian physicist and one of the pioneers of quantum mechanics. He is best known for his wave equation, which describes how the quantum state of a physical system changes over time, and his famous thought experiment, "Schrödinger's cat." Schrödinger was awarded the Nobel Prize in Physics in 1933 for his contributions to quantum theory. Despite his significant scientific achievements, Schrödinger maintained a lifelong interest in philosophy and the deeper questions of consciousness and reality.

Two Thoughts from
REID HOFFMAN

"Remember: If you don't find risk, risk will find you."

"Ironically, in a changing world, playing it safe is one of the riskiest things you can do."

Reid Hoffman is an American entrepreneur, venture capitalist, and author. He is best known as the cofounder of LinkedIn, the world's largest professional networking site. He has also invested in notable companies like Facebook, Airbnb, and Zynga. Hoffman is a partner at the venture capital firm Greylock Partners and has authored several books in which he shares his insights on career development and business growth. These include *Blitzscaling* (co-authored with Chris Yeh) and *The Start-Up of You*.

Two Thoughts from

W. EDWARDS DEMING

"If you can't describe what you are doing as a process, you don't know what you're doing."

"Without data, you're just another person with an opinion."

W. Edwards Deming was an American statistician, professor, author, and consultant widely recognized for his work in quality control and management. He is best known for his role in Japan's post–World War II economic recovery, where he implemented innovative management and collaborative techniques that helped spur rapid industrial growth. Deming's methods influenced a business management philosophy known as Total Quality Management (TQM), which is still relevant today.

Two Thoughts from

KUNAL SHAH

"Show me an easily offended person, and I will show you a person with deep insecurities."

"Replace the time spent discussing other people with any other topic and see your life get better in no time."

Kunal Shah is an Indian entrepreneur, investor, and speaker, best known as the founder of Freecharge, a mobile recharge platform, which was acquired by Snapdeal in 2015 for over $400 million. He is considered a pioneer in furthering the mobile commerce revolution in India. Currently, he is the founder and CEO of CRED, a digital platform that rewards people for paying their credit card bills on time. Shah is also known for his insights on human behavior, psychology, and productivity.

Two Thoughts from
STEVE JOBS

"One way to remember who you are is to remember who your heroes are."

"If today were the last day of my life, would I want to do what I am about to do today?"

Steve Jobs was an American entrepreneur, marketer, and inventor. A pioneer in the technology industry, Jobs cofounded Apple Inc., NeXT Inc., and Pixar Animation Studios and contributed significantly to the creation of various devices such as the iPhone, iPad, iPod, and the Macintosh computer. He was known for his unique management and leadership styles, as well as his emphasis on design and aesthetics.

Two Thoughts from

RUPERT SHELDRAKE

"Science at its best is an open-minded method of inquiry, not a belief system."

"Strategic thinking requires the ability to contemplate possibilities that are not immediately present."

Rupert Sheldrake is a British biologist and author best known for his hypothesis of "morphic resonance"—a concept that suggests a universal life force that governs forms and behaviors across time and space. Sheldrake's ideas have often been met with controversy and skepticism within the scientific community, but his work has inspired discussions on the boundaries of scientific inquiry and new paradigms of understanding. In addition to his scientific pursuits, Sheldrake has written numerous books exploring consciousness, parapsychology, and alternative theories.

Two Thoughts from

LYNN MARGULIS

"Life did not take over the world by combat, but by networking."

"Evolution is no linear family tree, but change in the single multidimensional being that has grown to cover the entire surface of Earth."

Lynn Margulis was an American evolutionary theorist, biologist, and author. Her groundbreaking work on the endosymbiotic theory explained the origin of eukaryotic cells through the symbiosis of bacterial lineages. She also developed the Serial Endosymbiotic Theory, which further explored symbiotic relationships between living organisms. Margulis was awarded the National Medal of Science in 1999 for her contributions to the field.

Two Thoughts from
SEBASTIAN JUNGER

"Humans don't mind hardship, in fact they thrive on it; what they mind is not feeling necessary."

"As modern society reduced the role of community, it simultaneously elevated the role of authority."

Sebastian Junger is an American journalist, author, and documentary filmmaker. He is best known for his book *The Perfect Storm* and the documentary film *Restrepo*, which earned an Academy Award nomination for Best Documentary Feature. Junger's work primarily focuses on the experiences of war and its impact on individuals and communities. In his book *Tribe*, he explores the connections between warfare, humans' innate need for community, and the decline of community in modern society.

Two Thoughts from

JOHANNES KEPLER

"I much prefer the sharpest criticism of a single intelligent man to the thoughtless approval of the masses."

"Nature uses as little as possible of anything."

Johannes Kepler was a German astronomer and mathematician. He was also a key figure of the Scientific Revolution; his contributions included advancements in optics, such as the explanation of how the human eye perceives images. He is most famous for his idea that the planets move in elliptical, rather than circular, orbits and that their movements in these orbits are governed by a set of laws, which became known as Kepler's laws of planetary motion.

Two Thoughts from
TOM WOLFE

"An intellectual is a person knowledgeable in one field who speaks out only in others."

"A cult is a religion with no political power."

Tom Wolfe was an American author and journalist known for his innovative and influential writing style in fiction and nonfiction. With works like *The Electric Kool-Aid Acid Test*, *The Right Stuff*, and *Bonfire of the Vanities*, he helped to pioneer the New Journalism movement and became one of America's most prominent literary figures. Wolfe's distinctive style combined traditional reporting with literary techniques, often using a satirical lens to highlight societal issues.

Two Thoughts from

NAVAL RAVIKANT

"Reading is the ultimate meta-skill that can be traded for anything else."

"Don't partner with pessimists, partner with rational optimists."

Naval Ravikant is an Indian American entrepreneur, investor, and author. Ravikant cofounded AngelList, a platform that connects start-ups and angel investors, and has invested in more than 100 companies, including Twitter and Uber. He is an influential voice in the areas of personal growth, mental health, and wealth creation. Ravikant has a vast following on social media and is known for his insightful quotes, interviews, and podcasts aimed at guiding others toward success and happiness.

Two Thoughts from
ROLF DOBELLI

"If 50 million people say something foolish, it is still foolish."

"It is much more common that we overestimate our knowledge than that we underestimate it."

Rolf Dobelli is a Swiss business author and entrepreneur best known for his best-selling book *The Art of Thinking Clearly*, which has been translated into 30+ languages. Dobelli is the founder of WORLD.MINDS, a community of leading international thinkers and scientists, and has also authored several other books on decision-making, human behavior, and cognitive biases. In addition to his writing career, Dobelli was a former CFO and board member of various Swiss corporations.

Two Thoughts from
WILL STORR

"We typically have a bias that tells us we are less susceptible to bias than everyone else."

"Intelligence is no protection against strange beliefs."

Will Storr is an award-winning British journalist and author known for his thought-provoking books on various topics, including self-help and the science of storytelling. His works, such as *The Status Game* and *The Science of Storytelling*, delve into the human mind, investigating cognitive biases and exploring the ways we create narratives to make sense of the world. Storr has also written for various publications, including the *Guardian*, the *Sunday Times*, and the *New Yorker*.

Two Thoughts from

RUDY RUCKER

"All living things are gnarly, in that they inevitably do things that are much more complex than one might have expected."

"One of the nice things about science fiction is that it lets us carry out thought experiments."

Rudy Rucker is an American mathematician, computer scientist, and science fiction author best known for his work in the cyberpunk subgenre. He is also a pioneer in the field of cellular automata and has made significant contributions to the study of infinity. Rucker has a unique writing style, blending heavy concepts like mathematics, computer science, and philosophy into his wildly imaginative stories.

Two Thoughts from
TOM STANDAGE

"It is a sign of a medium's immaturity when one of the main topics of discussion is the medium itself."

"Collectively, Europe's coffeehouses functioned as the Internet of the Age of Reason."

Tom Standage is a British journalist and author currently serving as the deputy editor of *The Economist*. In tandem with his journalistic work, Standage has published six books, the most recent being *A Brief History of Motion*. Writing aside, Standage is the drummer for the band Sebastopol.

Two Thoughts from
LEWIS WOLPERT

"I regard it as ethically unacceptable and impractical to censor any aspect of trying to understand the nature of our world."

"I strongly hold that, if an idea fits with common sense, then scientifically it is almost certain to be false."

Lewis Wolpert was a South African–born British biologist and author best known for his French flag model of embryonic development. Wolpert published over 200 scientific articles over the course of his career as well as several books, for which he received numerous accolades, including a Michael Faraday Medal and Prize from the Institute of Physics, a Royal Medal from the Royal Society, and a CBE from Queen Elizabeth II.

Two Thoughts from
REBECCA WEST

"Writing has nothing to do with communication between person and person, only with communication between different parts of a person's mind."

"It is always one's virtues and not one's vices that precipitate one into disaster."

Rebecca West was a British author and journalist best known for her reporting during the Nürnberg trials and for her advocacy for women's suffrage. Described by *Time* magazine as "indisputably the world's number one woman writer" in 1947, West authored over 20 books and was a contributing writer to several magazines such as the *New Yorker* and the *Times*. West was awarded a CBE in 1949 and a DBE in 1959.

Two Thoughts from

FRITJOF CAPRA

"The phenomenon of emergence takes place at critical points of instability that arise from fluctuations in the environment, amplified by feedback loops."

"Patterns cannot be weighed or measured. Patterns must be mapped."

Fritjof Capra is an Austrian American physicist and systems theorist, as well as the founding director of the Center for Ecoliteracy in Berkeley, California. Capra is the author of several books, most notably *The Tao of Physics* and *The Turning Point*, which attempt to bridge the gap between physics and metaphysics. Capra is fluent in German, English, French, and Italian.

Two Thoughts from
BEN GOLDACRE

"I spend a lot of time talking to people who disagree with me—I would go so far as to say that it's my favourite leisure activity."

"You are a placebo responder. Your body plays tricks on your mind. You cannot be trusted."

Ben Goldacre is a British physician and writer best known for his "Bad Science" column in the *Guardian*. Journalism aside, Goldacre is the author of four books, including *Bad Science*, an examination of irrationality, particularly within alternative medicine, and *Bad Pharma*, a critique of the pharmaceutical industry. Goldacre is the first Bennett Professor of Evidence-Based Medicine at the University of Oxford.

Two Thoughts from

GREGORY BATESON

"Rigor alone is paralytic death, but imagination alone is insanity."

"We are most of us governed by epistemologies that we know to be wrong."

Gregory Bateson was an English scientist and cyberneticist whose work interwove anthropology, sociology, and semiotics. An early student of systems theory, Bateson was one of the core members of the famous Macy Conferences on Cybernetics (1941–1960). The author of several acclaimed books, such as *Steps to an Ecology of Mind*, Bateson and his colleagues also developed the double-bind theory of schizophrenia.

Two Thoughts from
GEORGE CHURCH

"Every disease that's with us is caused by DNA. And every disease can be fixed by DNA."

"I have faith that science is a good thing. I am in awe of nature. In fact, I think to some extent, 'awe' was a word that was almost invented for scientists."

George Church is an American geneticist and entrepreneur currently serving as the Robert Winthrop Professor of Genetics at Harvard University. Operating out of his lab at Harvard, Church has cofounded around 50 biotech companies thus far, setting a record by spinning off 16 biotech companies in one year. In 2017, *Time* magazine listed Church as one of the 100 most influential people in the world.

Two Thoughts from

E. O. WILSON

"To the extent that philosophical positions both confuse us and close doors to further inquiry, they are likely to be wrong."

"If history and science have taught us anything, it is that passion and desire are not the same as truth."

E. O. Wilson was an American biologist and author known for developing the field of sociobiology. A multiple-time *New York Times* best-selling author, Wilson was also a two-time winner of the Pulitzer Prize for General Nonfiction for *On Human Nature* and *The Ants*. Writing aside, Wilson served as the curator of entomology at Harvard's Museum of Comparative Zoology for more than 20 years.

Two thoughts from
AMY MORIN

"Learning from each mistake requires self-awareness and humility, but it can be one of the biggest keys to reaching your full potential."

"Each time you avoid saying no to something you really don't want, you give away your power."

Amy Morin is an American psychotherapist and author who currently lectures at Northeastern University. Her books *13 Things Mentally Strong People Don't Do* and *13 Things Mentally Strong Parents Don't Do*, both international bestsellers, have been translated into more than 30 languages. Morin's TEDx talk, "The Secret of Becoming Mentally Strong," quickly became one of the top 25 talks of all time, with over 9 million views to date.

Two Thoughts from
JOEL GARREAU

"The essence of being human is being creative."

"The next frontier is our own selves."

Joel Garreau is an American journalist and writer best known as the author of *The Nine Nations of North America* and *Radical Change*. Having previously served as a fellow at Cambridge University and a Bernard L. Schwartz Fellow at New America Foundation, Garreau became the Lincoln Professor of Law, Culture and Values at Arizona State University in 2010. Previously, Garreau was a longtime reporter and editor at the *Washington Post*.

Two Thoughts from

GIDEON RACHMAN

"Durable political systems ultimately rely on institutions, not individuals."

"Asian nationalism is driven by rising expectations; the West's nationalism is driven by disappointed hopes."

Gideon Rachman is a British journalist and author who became the chief foreign affairs commentator for the *Financial Times* in 2006. Rachman's first book, *Zero-Sum World*, was met with much critical acclaim and has since been translated into seven languages. In addition to winning the Orwell Prize and the European Press Prize, Rachman was named foreign commentator of the year in Britain's Comment Awards in 2010.

Two Thoughts from
PEDRO DOMINGOS

"It's not man versus machine; it's man with machine versus man without. Data and intuition are like horse and rider, and you don't try to outrun a horse; you ride it."

"Bias is a learner's tendency to consistently learn the same wrong thing."

Pedro Domingos is a Portuguese AI researcher and author of the worldwide bestseller *The Master Algorithm*. A professor emeritus of computer science at the University of Washington, Domingos has received both the SIGKDD Innovation Award and the IJCAI John McCarthy Award, two of the highest honors in data science and AI. Outside of academia, Domingos has written for the *Wall Street Journal*, *Scientific American*, *Wired*, and others.

Two Thoughts from

APRIL DUNFORD

"Understanding something new is challenging because we don't yet have a frame of reference."

"If we fail at positioning, we fail at marketing and sales. If we fail at marketing and sales, the entire business fails."

April Dunford is a Canadian start-up executive and author. She is best known for her book *Obviously Awesome*. Throughout her 25-year career, Dunford led teams at seven successful B2B technology start-ups, whose acquisitions totaled over $2 billion. Today, Dunford splits her time between consulting and writing, as well as hosting the *Positioning* podcast.

Two Thoughts from
DAVID ROBSON

"What we feel and think will determine what we experience, which will in turn influence what we feel and what we think, in a never-ending cycle."

"The same qualities that will make you learn more productively also make you reason more wisely."

David Robson is a British science writer specializing in the extremes of the human brain, body, and behavior. In addition to writing for the likes of the *Guardian* and the *Atlantic*, Robson has published several books, most notably *The Expectation Effect*, which received a British Psychological Society Book Award. For his writing on misinformation and risk communication during the COVID pandemic, Robson received awards from the Association of British Science Writers and the UK Medical Journalists' Association.

Two Thoughts from
JON GERTNER

"In any company's greatest achievements one might, with the clarity of hindsight, locate the beginnings of its own demise."

"But to an innovator, being early is not necessarily different from being wrong."

Jon Gertner is an American journalist and historian whose explorations of science and nature have appeared in the *New York Times* and the *Wall Street Journal*, among others. Gertner's first book, *The Idea Factory*, was a *New York Times* bestseller. While researching his second book, *The Ice at the End of the World*, Gertner slept alongside glaciers, drank from meltwater streams, and accompanied NASA teams measuring Greenland's ice sheet.

Two Thoughts from

WALTER BAGEHOT

"Public opinion is a permeating influence, and it exacts obedience to itself; it requires us to drink other men's thoughts, to speak other men's words, to follow other men's habits."

"Life is a school of probability."

Walter Bagehot was an English journalist and essayist who wrote extensively about government, economics, and literature. A celebrated editor of *The Economist*, Bagehot also cofounded *National Review* in 1855. His major works include *The English Constitution* and *Lombard Street: A Description of the Money Market*.

Two Thoughts from
PER BAK

"An unlikely event is likely to happen because there are so many unlikely events that could happen."

"You don't get rich from doing physics, but you do get an opportunity to go to all the places the rich would go to if they had the time."

Per Bak was a Danish theoretical physicist best known for his theory of "self-organized criticality." Bak pursued his theory's implications at several institutions, including the Santa Fe Institute and Imperial College London, where he became a professor in 2000. In 1996, Bak took his ideas to a broader audience with his popular book *How Nature Works*.

Two Thoughts from

DOUGLAS R. HOFSTADTER

"For now, what is important is not finding the answer, but looking for it."

"It is curious, how one often mistrusts one's own opinions if they are stated by someone else."

Douglas R. Hofstadter is an American physicist and writer. He is best known for his book *Gödel, Escher, Bach*, which received the Pulitzer Prize for General Nonfiction. The author of multiple books on consciousness, analogies, mathematics, and art, Hofstadter also wrote a popular column for *Scientific American* entitled "Metamagical Themas." On April 3, 1995, Hofstadter's book *Fluid Concepts and Creative Analogies* was the first book sold on Amazon.

Two Thoughts from
LEWIS THOMAS

"The future is too interesting and dangerous to be entrusted to any predictable, reliable agency."

"The capacity to blunder slightly is the real marvel of DNA. Without it, we would still be anaerobic bacteria and there would be no music."

Lewis Thomas was an esteemed American physician and writer. He is best known for his reflective essays on human biology and the human condition. His award-winning writings made him a notable voice in scientific literature, bridging the gap between complex scientific principles and general public understanding. Even as he was dying, he discussed death with Roger Rosenblatt, reportedly saying, "There's really no such thing as the agony of dying."

Two Thoughts from
LINUS PAULING

"Satisfaction of one's curiosity is one of the greatest sources of happiness in life."

"In teaching, you do not want to cover things, you want to uncover them. The best way to get good ideas is to have lots of ideas."

Linus Pauling was an American chemist and peace activist who published more than 1,200 papers and books over the course of his life. Pauling is the only person to have been awarded two unshared Nobel Prizes, receiving the Nobel Prize in Chemistry in 1954 and the Nobel Peace Prize in 1962. *New Scientist* named Pauling as one of the 20 greatest scientists of all time.

Two Thoughts from
FEI-FEI LI

"If our era is the next Industrial Revolution, as many claim, AI is surely one of its driving forces."

"Understanding vision and building visual systems is really understanding intelligence."

Fei-Fei Li is a Chinese-born American computer scientist and expert in AI, particularly in the field of computer vision. She is a professor at Stanford University and the codirector of Stanford's Human-Centered Artificial Intelligence Institute. She was the leading scientist and principal investigator of ImageNet, a dataset that greatly influenced the development of deep learning. A firm advocate for diversity in technology, Li cofounded AI4ALL, a nonprofit organization aimed at increasing underrepresented minorities in the AI industry.

Two Thoughts from

DAVID EPSTEIN

"You have people walking around with all the knowledge of humanity on their phone, but they have no idea how to integrate it. We don't train people in thinking or reasoning."

"We learn who we are in practice, not in theory."

David Epstein is an American journalist and author. He is best known as the author of *Range* and *The Sports Gene*, both *New York Times* bestsellers. Along with the likes of ProPublica and *Sports Illustrated*, Epstein's work has been included in the *Best American Science and Nature Writing* anthology. Today, Epstein serves on the board of directors of Jubilee JumpStart, an early childhood education center focused on families with the least access.

Two Thoughts from

GEORG LICHTENBERG

"You can make a good living from soothsaying but not from truthsaying."

"The most dangerous of all falsehoods is a slightly distorted truth."

Georg Lichtenberg was a German physicist and aphorist. He is widely considered to be the founder of experimental physics in Germany. In 1777, Lichtenberg discovered the basic principle of modern xerographic copying, whose images are still referred to as "Lichtenberg figures." From 1765 until the end of his life, Lichtenberg kept a series of notebooks entitled *Sudelbücher*, or "scrapbooks," selections of which remain in print to this day.

TWO CONCLUDING THOUGHTS

Some of the ideas in this book may have propelled your Prover into overdrive. This is natural: we are, after all, only human.

But have you noticed a different voice emerging? Where your Prover once enjoyed unrivaled dominion, you may have begun to hear the Thinker's clarion call slicing through the noise, its presence heralded by just one single, persistent question: *Why*?

When your Thinker awakens, you may notice that the world begins to look different. What once seemed obvious may now seem insane. What once seemed insane may now seem obvious.

The transformation is ongoing. As you evolve, your beliefs will too, anchored not in dogma or emotion, but in curiosity and the search for truth.

And remember—as you step into the new world, this book will be right by your side, not as an artifact on your bookshelf or collecting dust on your coffee table, but as a companion. Whenever your Prover begins to cloak your worldview in the comfortable blanket of consensus, these pages await to bring your Thinker back to life.

* * *

The American writer Tom Peters (who you may recognize from the Scholars section of this book) once remarked, "If I read a book that cost me $20 and I got one idea, I've gotten one of the greatest bargains of all time."

Insightful, yet incomplete.

It's one thing to uncover an idea; its true value, however, is realized only through its execution.

If this book has served its purpose, you now stand at a crossroads, armed with far more than just one idea (500, to be exact).

Each page, each line in this book was crafted to challenge, inspire, and incite.

The real question is not what you've learned, but rather, what will you do with it?

NOTES

1. https://www.infiniteloopspodcast.com/
2. https://newsletter.osv.llc/
3. https://quoteinvestigator.com/2014/11/18/great-minds/
4. Likely misattributed.
   https://quoteinvestigator.com/2014/09/09/worry-less/
5. Likely misattributed.
   https://quoteinvestigator.com/2015/11/01/cure/
6. This saying has been used by Anaïs Nin, but origin is not known.
   https://quoteinvestigator.com/2014/03/09/as-we-are/
7. Likely misattributed.
   Multiple sources credit it to Dixy Lee Ray as well.
8. Likely misattributed.
   https://www.usatoday.com/story/news/factcheck/2021/05/04/fact-check-quote-attributed-virginia-woolf-movie/4935521001/
9. Likely misattributed.
   https://quoteinvestigator.com/2018/12/03/open-door/
10. Likely misattributed.
    https://thoughtcatalog.com/?p=371449
11. Likely misattributed.
    https://quoteinvestigator.com/2021/11/03/not-buried/
12. Likely misattributed.
    https://quoteinvestigator.com/2016/06/26/shape/
13. Likely misattributed.
    https://quoteinvestigator.com/2011/10/28/judge-character/
14. Likely misattributed.
    https://quoteinvestigator.com/2015/07/04/seen/

INDEX OF THINKERS

Abumrad, Jad 152
Adams, Samuel 211
Aeschylus 37
Agrawal, Ajay 128
Alexander the Great 197
Ali, Muhammad 136
Allen, James 194
Armstrong, Louis 165
Aurelius, Marcus 174
Bacon, Francis 188
Bagehot, Walter 273
Bak, Per 274
Bakunin, Mikhail 226
Barnes, Julian 62
Bateson, Gregory 263
Baudrillard, Jean 132
Beckett, Samuel 48
Benkler, Yochai 127
Bogle, Jack 96
Bowie, David 149
Brown, Margaret Wise 68
Brown, Derren 162
Brown, Brené 210
Bruce, Lenny 168
Bryson, Bill 56
Bukowski, Charles 57
Burgess, Anthony 29
Burns, Ken 160

Bush, Barbara 220
Camus, Albert 182
Capra, Fritjof 261
Carnegie, Dale 108
Cattell, Raymond 100
Chekhov, Anton 41
Church, George 264
Clausewitz, Carl von 191
Cleese, John 159
Cocteau, Jean 223
Cohen, Leonard 147
Crick, Francis 238
Crowley, Aleister 164
Curie, Marie 236
Czerski, Helen 243
Darwin, Charles 103
Davis, Wade 88
Debord, Guy 215
Deming, W. Edwards 246
Dick, Philip K. 45
Dickinson, Emily 36
Diderot, Denis 186
Dobelli, Rolf 255
Domingos, Pedro 269
Dostoevsky, Fyodor 33
Duke, Annie 142
Dunford, April 270
Dylan, Bob 139

Easwaran, Eknath 203
Egan, Jennifer 60
Einstein, Albert 230
Ekman, Paul 82
Ellison, Ralph 64
Emerson, Ralph Waldo 66
Epictetus 180
Epstein, David 279
Euripides 59
Franck, Frederick 166
Frankl, Viktor 86
Franklin, Benjamin 177
Frederick the Great 205
Freud, Sigmund 104
Frey, Thomas 221
Friedman, Milton 81
Fritz, Robert 121
Fry, Stephen 157
Fuller, Margaret 39
Gaiman, Neil 23
Galbraith, John Kenneth 120
Gandhi, Mahatma 185
Garreau, Joel 267
George, Henry 113
Gertner, Jon 272
Gibbon, Edward 105
Gibran, Kahlil 25
Glaeser, Edward 106

Gleick, James 124
Goethe, Johann Wolfgang von 214
Goggins, David 204
Goldacre, Ben 262
Goldsmith, Oliver 53
Gracián, Baltasar 224
Graham, Benjamin 87
Gray, Peter 89
Haidt, Jonathan 109
Harari, Yuval Noah 110
Harburg, Yip 141
Hardy, Benjamin P. 119
Havel, Václav 222
Hawking, Stephen 241
Hayek, Friedrich 93
Hecht, Ben 170
Heine, Heinrich 32
Heinlein, Robert A. 22
Hemingway, Ernest 26
Heraclitus 200
Hightower, Jim 196
Hitchens, Christopher 237
Hitz, Zena 111
Hoffman, Reid 245
Hofstadter, Douglas R. 275
Hosseini, Khaled 43
Housel, Morgan 47
Howard, Robert E. 73

Humboldt, Alexander von 183
Hunt, Lynn 129
Huxley, Aldous 34
Irving, John 28
Iyer, Pico 69
Jami, Criss 219
Jeffers, Robinson 38
Jefferson, Thomas 198
Jobs, Steve 248
Johnson, Samuel 61
Jones, Gayl 52
Jordan, Michael 158
Junger, Sebastian 251
Kafka, Franz 67
Kahneman, Daniel 91
Kasparov, Garry 138
Keller, Helen 80
Kent, Corita 156
Kepler, Johannes 252
Kerouac, Jack 54
Keynes, John Maynard 97
Kierkegaard, Søren 207
Kreider, Tim 35
Kross, Ethan 126
Landes, David 99
Langer, Susanne 122
Lennon, John 161
Leonardo da Vinci 178

Levy, Marv 151
Lewin, Kurt 130
Lewis, C. S. 75
Li, Fei-Fei 278
Lichtenberg, Georg 280
Lovecraft, H. P. 49
MacLeod, Hugh 167
Madison, James 202
Mandela, Nelson 190
Mantel, Hilary 63
Margulis, Lynn 250
Martin, Roger L. 85
Maslow, Abraham 112
Maugham, W. Somerset 65
McConaughey, Matthew 137
McKenna, Terence 107
McLuhan, Marshall 209
Meir, Golda 201
Merton, Robert K. 84
Midgley, Mary 193
Mises, Ludwig von 102
Monroe, Marilyn 163
Montaigne, Michel de 218
Moravia, Alberto 71
Morgan, J. P. 233
Morin, Amy 266
Munger, Charlie 92
Musashi, Miyamoto 148

Neumann, John von 242
Nietzsche, Friedrich 176
Nin, Anaïs 40
Nolan, Christopher 154
O'Keeffe, Georgia 140
Ortega y Gasset, José 216
Paglia, Camille 90
Paine, Thomas 184
Painter, Nell Irvin 83
Parker, Dorothy 21
Parks, Rosa 175
Pauling, Linus 277
Peters, Tom 131
Popper, Karl 213
Postman, Neil 42
Pulley, Natasha 70
Pynchon, Thomas 44
Quevedo, Francisco de 58
Rachman, Gideon 268
Ravikant, Naval 254
Robson, David 271
Rogan, Joe 145
Rohn, Jim 206
Roosevelt, Eleanor 187
Rosling, Hans 117
Rovelli, Carlo 231
Rucker, Rudy 257
Ruiz, Don Miguel 181

Ruiz Zafón, Carlos 31
Rushdie, Salman 50
Ruth, Babe 150
Ryle, Gilbert 217
Sartre, Jean-Paul 55
Schelling, Friedrich 212
Schopenhauer, Arthur 179
Schrödinger, Erwin 244
Schweitzer, Albert 199
Sethi, Ramit 118
Shah, Kunal 247
Sheldrake, Rupert 249
Simon, Paul 146
Simon, Herbert A. 234
Singer, Michael A. 195
Slingerland, Edward 123
Soth, Alec 169
Spielberg, Steven 144
Standage, Tom 258
Steinbeck, John 51
Stendhal 76
Storr, Will 256
Strayed, Cheryl 24
Stutz, Phil 116
Swart, Tara 232
Szasz, Thomas 101
Tapscott, Don 114
Tartt, Donna 74

Templeton, Sir John 94
Tesla, Nikola 235
Thiel, Peter 240
Thomas, Lewis 276
Thompson, Hunter S. 239
Tolkien, J. R. R. 72
Tolstoy, Leo 27
Tracy, Brian 225
Vowell, Sarah 125
Walker, Alice 30
Wallace, David Foster 20
Ward, William Arthur 189
Washington, Booker T. 115
Washington, Denzel 143
Watterson, Bill 171
West, Mae 153
West, Rebecca 260
Wilson, E. O. 265
Wolfe, Tom 253
Wolpert, Lewis 259
Woolf, Virginia 46
Wrangham, Richard 95
Wu, Tim 98
Zappa, Frank 155
Zhuang, Zhou (Zhuangzi) 192
Žižek, Slavoj 208

ABOUT THE CURATORS

Jim O'Shaughnessy built O'Shaughnessy Asset Management (OSAM) into a Wall Street powerhouse, managing billions before its successful acquisition. Now he's embarked on a new venture: O'Shaughnessy Ventures (OSV), a creative investment firm empowering visionaries across business, tech, science, art, media, and literature.

Hailed as a "legendary investor" by *Barron's*, Jim is the author of the New York Times bestseller *What Works on Wall Street* and three other influential books. His expertise spans quantitative analysis, portfolio management, and investment strategy.

Beyond finance, Jim has served as former chair of the Chamber Music Society of Lincoln Center and host of the popular Infinite Loops podcast. He shares eclectic insights on everything from philosophy to quantum mechanics via his active X presence (@jposhaughnessy). Jim resides in Connecticut with his wife Melissa, surrounded by the joyful chaos of their three children and six grandchildren.

Vatsal Kaushik is an entrepreneur and engineer who builds at the intersection of technology and culture. Since 2017, he has launched multiple ventures, including the startup WebSqill and the book recommendation platform The Antilibrary.

As a key member of O'Shaughnessy Ventures, Vatsal helped launch the company and its popular Infinite Loops podcast. He's currently building **OSV's publishing imprint**, Infinite Books.

Vatsal lives in Dehradun, India with his wife, Manu. He shares his thoughts on books, technology, and ideas on X @vtslkshk.

ABOUT INFINITE BOOKS

Infinite Books crafts excellent books written by exceptional authors. We publish works that stand the test of time—as relevant a century from now as they are today.

From fiction to nonfiction, poetry to prose, Infinite Books strives to be a beacon of clarity in a world full of noise. Our authors receive meticulous editorial support from a team fiercely devoted to their success, and we focus on good ideas that tell a compelling story and ignite a spark. We're rethinking the publishing model for the modern era, from concept to execution, editing to design and marketing.

To learn more and join our mission, visit www.infinitebooks.com or scan the QR code below.

Made in the USA
Middletown, DE
23 March 2025